PRAISE FO

Thirty to

"Who knew planning a wedding could actually be funny? Michaels does that and even more as he takes us all on the journey from guys' guy to groom. Helpful, funny, but most of all honest . . . a great peek into the mind of an almost-married man."

—JENNY LEE, author of *I Do. I Did. Now What?!*
Life After the Wedding Dress

"Most ... on fluff, ... so Craig ... gly practic ... is a simple ... irl- wind ... be must-

"Buyi ... er. Trust ... m- to-be."

"Besid ... will energi ... ed- ding. ... for ... nal

THIRTY TO WIFE

ABOUT THE AUTHOR

CRAIG MICHAELS, a graduate of the University of Virginia and Northwestern's Kellogg School of Management, is a happily married man, but the memory of his wedding planning is still fresh in his mind. Craig owns and operates Groom411.com, an extensive Web site serving as a sounding board to help grooms not make the same mistakes he did. Craig lives in the San Francisco Bay Area with his wife, Debora, and Lucy, their Labrador.

If you have a groom suggestion, comment, or just want to say hi, contact Craig at Craig@Groom411.com.

THIRTY TO WIFE

THE TELL-ALL
GROOM'S GUIDE TO WEDDINGS—
HOW TO GET HITCHED WITHOUT
LOSING YOUR MIND OR
YOUR FIANCÉE

Craig Michaels

MARLOWE & COMPANY
NEW YORK

THIRTY TO WIFE:
The Tell-All Groom's Guide to Weddings—How to Get Hitched
without Losing Your Mind or Your Fiancée
Copyright © 2006 by Craig Michaels
Foreword copyright © 2006 by Debora Halloran Michaels

Published by
Marlowe & Company
An Imprint of Avalon Publishing Group, Incorporated
245 West 17th Street • 11th Floor
New York, NY 10011-5300

AVALON

This memoir is the product of the author's recollections and is thus rendered
as a subjective accounting of events that occurred in his or her life.

Library of Congress Cataloging-in-Publication Data
Michaels, Craig A.
Thirty to wife : the tell-all groom's guide to weddings—how to get hitched without
losing your mind or your fiancée / Craig Michaels.
p. cm.
ISBN 1-56924-296-8
1. Weddings—Planning. 2. Bridegrooms. I. Title : Groom's guide to Weddings—
how to get hitched without losing your mind or your fiancée. II. Title.
HQ745.M653 2006
395.2'2—dc22   2005035682

ISBN-13: 978-1-56924-296-4

9 8 7 6 5 4 3 2 1

Designed by Pauline Neuwirth, Neuwirth & Associates, Inc.

Illustrations by Karen Paluska

Printed in the United States of America

TO DEB, WITH ALL MY HEART.

Contents

MARRIED LIFE DAY 1
WHAT HAPPENS IN VEGAS
IS LEGALLY RECOGNIZED IN EVERY OTHER STATE • 243

APPENDIX A
THE COMPLETE GUIDE TO THE
GROOM'S WEDDING TO-DO'S • 246

APPENDIX B
THE COMPLETE GUIDE TO THE GROOM'S
PARTY RESPONSIBILITIES • 258

DebWord

(aka a Foreword from Craig's wife, Deb)

IF ONLY CRAIG put a fraction of the effort into our wedding planning that he did writing this book.

If only.

I really hope you enjoy reading about Craig's misadventures and mistakes as my hopeless fiancé. While I'm not thrilled in everyone reading about what went right and, more often, what went wrong, as his wife, I am proud of his ability to turn a frustrating time for two ordinary people into a humorous story for many to delight in and learn something from.

To be honest, I'd prefer this book to be a love story and not a cautionary tale, but as you will find out, marriage is all about compromise. I'm saving that topic for my own book.

Craig asked me to share some advice with his female readers. Advice that didn't include canceling the wedding. Male readers will get more guidance than bargained for inside the book. So, for the ladies who are completely stunned that their Prince Charming has suddenly turned into a smelly toad, I offer these three simple rules:

* Give your fiancé manageable and accomplishable tasks and deadlines. Remember that men are problem-solvers.
* Don't let him off the hook for extended periods of time. Prevent him from underwhelming you.
* If he relents and still doesn't meet minimum expectations, make him read or re-read this book. Cover to cover. And say three times, "I won't pull a Craig."

Congratulations on your engagement and good luck with your wedding.

—Deb

P.S. Craig wasn't really *that* bad.
P.P.S. Craig added this after I turned in the text.
P.P.P.S. No I didn't.

Acknowledgments

I WOULD LIKE to thank Julie Burton for believing in me within ten seconds of my three-minute pitch; Lilly Ghahremani for being my biggest fan; Renée Sedliar for slicing and dicing like no one else; Karen Paluska for her designs; David Fitzpatrick, Paul Jacobson, Rick Wolfgram, Brian Maude, Bob Tollenaar, and all my friends for starring in my adventures and listening to my recaps over and over again; Mom, Dad, Jon, all my family, and my new in-laws for their never-ending support; our dog Lucy for serving as my always-available sounding board; and, of course, my wife, Deb, without whom this book and, more important, my life would not be the same, for (1) loving me enough to marry me and (2) loving me even more to allow me to share our story (okay, my version of our story).

Introduction

All tragedies are finished by a death.
All comedies are ended by a marriage.
(George Gordon, Lord Byron)

I SHOULD HAVE eloped. Plain and simple. Taken the money and run. Had my cake and actually eaten it, too. But that would have been too easy.

Most women have been planning their weddings since they were little girls. Guys? We can't plan toast without forgetting the bread.

Now, I'm different. My dream wedding has been etched in my brain for years. Instead of a guest list of hundreds, a big white canopy on a grassy field, miles of flowers, and a twenty-piece orchestra, my needs are much simpler. Man, woman, and license. Maybe add a pen and someone to pronounce us man and wife, but that's it. Cheap, quick, and with much lower blood pressures.

But I love my fiancée, Deb. She's smart and pretty, and we go great together. She is the one I want to marry, and she wanted a fairy-tale wedding. So, since life—or at least wedding planning—is full of compromises, I agreed to support Deb's grand vision.

How bad could it be?

Bad enough for me to write down my experience to help others better steer these treacherous engagement waters. So, read on. I implore you. And not just because I want to sell more books, although that's a good start.

You may be the first of your buddies to get married, like me, and face asking yourself, where's your Obi-Wan Kenobi? To whom should you turn for advice, comfort, and solace? Your fiancée? Your dad? Your bartender? I don't think so. And if you did already, let me guess their responses.

> **Fiancée:** "Don't you love me enough to figure this out on your own?"
>
> **Dad:** "Don't you love her enough to figure it own on your own?" (read: "How the hell should I know?")
>
> **Bartender:** "Another double vodka tonic?"

Or, maybe you're the group's last unmarried holdout and think, by now, you know it all. Or at least have seen it all. Don't flatter yourself. Unless you go through your own wedding or get a behind-the-scenes look like I'm about to give you, you're not privy to what really goes down. And out. And down further. And out the window. It doesn't matter that you've been a best man twice, a groomsman four times, slept with five bridesmaids, and bore more than your fair share of rings when you were eight. You're still going to need help figuring out your own wedding.

Now, I'm not a relationship expert. I don't have a PhD in human psychology. And I'm sure not a habitual groom. Once is enough for me. I'm an average guy. Not a metrosexual (although not for lack of trying). But, also, not a rabid NASCAR fan (although I do enjoy the tailgating). Just an average guy getting married. And doing a below-average job at it.

I looked at every groom guidebook out there. Actually, I had no choice. Deb bought them all and slipped some under my pillow, left a few in the bathroom, and voice-recorded the remaining ones to my iPod. But none of them told the whole story. In fact, most didn't tell any story. Just pages upon pages of responsibilities, requirements, and reasons why you have all those responsibilities and requirements. How's a red-blooded, short-attention-span man raised on MTV, Howard Stern, and five hundred television channels going to digest all of that? More important, why should you have to digest all of that?

You shouldn't. That's why you should listen to me.

Welcome to a chronicle of the last month of my single life.

Let's call it a self-imposed sentence of thirty days to wife, which will include the good, the bad, and, of course, the ugly. This isn't really a "how to" or "how not to" guide. Treat it more like a "you're not alone" handbook with a few wedding facts thrown in for you to impress your bride-to-be, girlfriend, or that stranger you just bought a drink for. (You lucky dog. Don't rush things.) And think of me not so much as a cautionary tale-teller, but as your guinea pig—going through the motions and making all the mistakes so you don't have to.

Aren't you lucky?

A COMPLETE GUIDE TO
THE GROOM'S WEDDING TO-DO'S

THIS PAGE INTENTIONALLY LEFT BLANK.

YES, THE LIST IS SO PAINFUL, I PUT IT IN THE APPENDIX.

1

I'M JUST GETTING STARTED.

One month to go

New to-do's

Wine and dine her

Plan a wedding-free moment by going to your favorite restaurant. Relive your first date. Or kiss. Or you-know-what. Ask how she's doing. And really listen. Don't race home to catch the end of the game. Or the latest episode of CSI. That's what TiVo is for. And if you don't have a TiVo, add it to your registry.

Old to-do's left to do

	How late am I?
Help choose bridal registry	8 months
Start honeymoon plans	8 months
Complete honeymoon plans	5 months
Order wedding rings	2 months
Attend dance lessons	2 months
Complete guest list	2 months
Shop for honeymoon clothes	2 months
Order wedding attire for self and groomsmen	2 months
Check marriage license requirements	2 months
Select gifts for bride and groomsmen	2 months
Help fiancée with Couple's Shower thank-you notes	2 months
Have bachelor party	2 months
Pick up wedding rings	2 months
Begin financial consolidation	2 months

WELCOME TO MY WORLD. SEATBELTS NOT REQUIRED, BUT STRONGLY ENCOURAGED.

> Bachelors should be heavily taxed.
> It's not fair that some men should be happier than others.
> (Oscar Wilde)

THE VEGAS SUN beats down on me. A slightly ill-fitting tux clings in all the wrong places. Two hundred eyes focus on my every move. My mom and dad tightly flank me. I'm staring down the barrel of the aisle.

It could be the dry heat that's keeping me from sweating through my tux, or maybe it's the two sticks of Right Guard I used this morning.

My mom is talking about how beautiful everything looks, but her words never fully reach my ears. Dad's peaceful silence screams volumes.

Who am I? Am I cut out to be someone's "husband?" Can I give up my fast and furious, living-on-the-edge lifestyle? Did my brother remember the ring? Did I confirm the honeymoon? Okay, now I'm scared. What do I do if I'm not equipped to actually take Deb's hand?

It's 4:30 AM. I can't sleep. It's been this way every morning for almost a year. Must not wake Deb. Pull arm from under head. Cross over Body. Tiptoe out door. Phew.

I feel my way to the couch, full of pity for our neighbors below as they receive yet another predawn stomping from above. Maybe I'll leave them a note today.

> Sorry for the noise, but I don't have long to live.
> I am getting married soon.
> Regards,
> Apartment 302

WE'VE BEEN ENGAGED for eight months. Dating for over two years, I've had more than enough time to "get off the pot," as it was eloquently put by some of my friends. And not just the female ones.

I popped the question on New Year's Eve. Deb wore a red dress. She always looks good in red. I wore my standard khakis. And for some reason Deb always thinks I look hot in them. An early tip that she was the one? Or a sign of severe vision impairment destined to be genetically passed down to future offspring?

Never was I so sure of anything in this world. Buoyed by excessive alcohol, a ticking biological clock (guys get them too), and a natural urge to ensure survival of the fittest (vision impairments aside), I got down on one knee and asked Deb to marry me.

It wasn't the most romantic moment. Or the most graceful. But it was ours to cherish forever. Or at least a few days.

"No planning for two months. Guaranteed," Deb promised as she basked in the glow of her engagement ring.

We didn't make it two hours.

"Who are your groomsmen?"

"What food should we serve?"

"Where should we honeymoon?"

"When will we register?"

Why, oh why did I start us down this path?

Then I remember Deb's comment way back on our fifteenth date. "You know I'm not dating for sport." I guess neither was I.

And I know that I haven't found much sport in planning our wedding. Successfully blowing off every responsibility is a challenge in and of itself. What's to stop me from finishing with a perfect record?

My blushing bride, for one.

If someone actually finds the woman who fancies the spontaneous city hall wedding over an elegant affair at the Top Of The Mark, he's found the one in the million (possibly billion). But the 99 percent of men on this planet should give in a little. Apply some effort. It won't hurt much, and there will be great rewards for the smallest of contributions. Why haven't I listened to *that* voice in my head and not the one saying "Dude, relax and stay clear of planning. You'll only mess it up"?

✧

I'VE BEEN SITTING on the couch for a few hours, awaiting Deb's wedding wrath (read: another reminder of today's to-do's). It really doesn't matter what I didn't do or what I need to do. The experience is the same (read: I'd rather have my teeth pulled).

Miraculously, no wrath. Just love and the opportunity to plead my case.

"You know I'm not a details guy. That's not why you fell for me," I offer.

"You better fucking become one," Deb counters. I've definitely brought out Deb's alter ego with all of this.

"No problem. New me. Starting today. Promise." Please don't pummel me.

Am I in denial? Am I ready? Is it only the wedding standing in my way of lifelong bliss?

Shouldn't I just stop bitching and look at the big picture? I want Deb. Deb wants wedding. Ergo, I want wedding. It's pretty simple. Only thirty days left.

But these thirty days are also my last remaining ones as a bachelor. As such, I feel compelled to squeeze as much out of this precious time as possible. It's not like I'm looking for a good time from every woman passing by. But this is it. Regardless of divorce statistics, once done, we're married. Years will pass like minutes. Or will minutes pass like years? I'll keep aging. And aging. And aging. And so will Deb. But that's a worry for another time. I'm already late for work.

✦

THE FIRST THING I do at the office is take an Emotional Inventory of all things Craig.

> How is Craig today?
> How can Craig better himself?
> What makes Craig feel good?
> What makes Craig feel bad?
> Does Craig treat others as Craig expects to be treated?
> Does Craig have an inner child yearning to be free?

Has Deb brainwashed me overnight? Has she switched my *Maxim* with her *Cosmopolitan* in an attempt to better prime me for marriage? This is bad. But no matter how hard I try, I can't stop. Because I must overcome my nagging PMS, land that great guy, and drop two dress sizes before next summer. I definitely have been reading the wrong articles. Regardless, I assess.

Good emotions	Bad emotions
Love	Cluelessness
Passion	Helplessness
Happiness	Sexlessness
Hopefulness	Empty pocketness

A tie. Not bad, given my circumstances. The sky isn't falling. Deb's call breaks my concentration. Or lack thereof.

My side of the conversation is always the same. "I promise. I'll take care of it. Yes, I am an asshole. No I won't be an asshole forever. I love you. No, I don't expect you to say it too."

Thanks to Deb, I remember to send a check to the invitation printers. Better late than never. In fact, those are the terms I have with all of our wedding vendors. Well, at least those are the terms I have with myself. Because once a vendor calls Deb asking why a payment is late, my tone quickly switches to "blood, firstborn, or direct withdrawal, whichever is easiest."

Mom calls next. No chance she's going to call me an asshole. Just checking to see how things are going, whether I'm eating well, and if there's a chance I'll be moving to New York any time soon. Typical mom stuff, repeated by typical moms everywhere. Alexander Graham Bell may have done wonders for interstate commerce by inventing the telephone, but he certainly didn't do any favors for us New York boys who have ventured westward, seeking sun, surf, and California babes. Sure it's tough when one's so far away. But, still, the calls can get a bit repetitive.

Maybe instead of shunning cross-country parental interactive technology, I should embrace it. High-definition Web cams (to make sure they're sure I'm getting enough rest). Networkable refrigerator barcode readers (to make sure I'm having enough broccoli). Real-time financial transaction tracking (to make sure I'm saving for a rainy day).

I'm positive once I have children, things will become a great deal clearer. And muddier. Clearer because I'll see me in my son or daughter and finally understand when parents say "wait until you have kids." Muddier because I'll see my parents in me. And realize how right they were. Will I then self-destruct like a robot that just received conflicting instructions (Must be cool dad. Must not let kid stay out late. Must not embarrass. Must protect. Danger. Danger.)?

Deb's friend and soon-to-be-bridesmaid Annie's call breaks my concentration. Or, still, lack thereof. "Tell me about Deb," she asks. Am I ever going to get work done today?

Deb's bridesmaids are preparing a quiz game for her bridal shower. Sounds harmless enough. I answer questions about my beloved and our relationship and, at the shower, they ask Deb the same questions. It could be cute. Or chaotic if we don't match many answers.

Luckily, this call constitutes the extent of my involvement in Deb's shower. A stark contrast to our Couple's Shower. Who invented that one? In the official rule of weddings, I am pretty sure this is an optional event, but "optional" doesn't seem to be in Deb's vocabulary lately.

✧

I WASN'T SURE what to expect from a Couple's Shower. Well, I had some ideas, but they were way off. No water. No lavender bubbles. No hot couples exploring their innermost fantasies. In the end, Deb and I both thought the Couple's Shower was fun, but for very different reasons. Deb loved talking about the wedding with friends and family. I got to drink beer with my buddies. The price I paid was playing a few feel-good games that no man would voluntarily participate in, like:

- **Touch your mate.** A blindfolded Deb had to identify me by touching body parts of the male partygoers. No, I didn't get a chance to do the same. No, Deb didn't pick me out. She mistook Joe, her sixty-year-old uncle, for me. Yes, I started going to the gym more.
- **Share candy, share story.** People innocently picked M&Ms from a jar and then were told that they had to tell as many Deb and Craig stories as they had M&Ms. Poor Patrick. His candy double-fisting took forty minutes to recover from. Even the M&Ms had enough. They melted in his hands after the third story.
- **Dress up.** Now it was my turn to be blindfolded. In front of everyone, I had to pull things out of a suitcase packed with possible wedding-night attire and try to put them on Deb. I figured out the teddy and slippers, but was a little stumped when it came to a diaphragm. "Why do we need an ashtray?"

In truth, some games were fun, others just mildly unpleasant. Just like our shower gifts. No offense to our gift givers, but just like the games, the booty was skewed on the feminine side. There were exceptions, namely the power drill and stainless steel barbeque tools. Not sure how to classify the tiger-print thong with

Velcro quick-release. A gift from Deb's mom. Enough said. Actually, way too much said.

✧

I SUCK AT Annie's questions.

> "What's Deb's favorite color?"
> "What's her best feature?"
> "What's the most romantic thing you two have done?"
> "When did Deb fall in love with you?"
> "When did you fall in love with Deb?"

My world slows, chest pounds, legs wobble, and eyes blur. Who cares about Annie's questions? What about my questions? Is Deb really the one for me? What do I really know about her? What do I know about myself? When will I feel my toes again?

"Are you still there?" Annie sounds worried. Rightly so.

"Green. Eyes. Naked Scrabble. Fifth date. Ditto. Gotta go. Bye."

ARE YOUR TO-DO'S NOT TO-DONE YET?

DID YOU SKIP a date with your fiancée, and aren't sure what to tell her?

Want to duck out of a meeting with your wedding planner?

Can't stand another visit with your future in-laws?

Try one of these excuses on for size.

- ❥ Someone's got to wash the dog.*
- ❥ You're a much better judge of that.
- ❥ Can't your mother take my place?*
- ❥ Can't someone gay take my place?
- ❥ I have to meet my parole officer. I'll explain later.
- ❥ I'll only upset you.

- They're replaying Super Bowl XII. You know how much I love the Cowboys.
- I have to give blood.*
- I had to help someone fix a flat. No she wasn't cute.
- I want to be surprised.*
- How much is that going to cost me?
- I'll go, but as long as you agree to pigs in blankets.
- My horoscope says I shouldn't make decisions today.*
- I should finalize my divorce first.*
- I have a restraining order at that store.*
- I hurt myself at the gym. Yes, the gym.
- Male problems.
- I got into a fistfight. It hurts, but you should see your dad.*
- The wedding planner made a pass at me the last time.
- It's against my religion.*
- I decided to wear my prom tux.
- I'm not good enough for you.
- Can't we just cuddle instead?
- I have to visit my mom. Maybe she can join us?*
- I'll be with you in spirit.*

*These excuses can also be used by brides-to-be. Although, I am not sure why any bride would need an excuse not to do wedding planning, but hey, I'm an equal opportunity procrastinator.

No explicit or implicit guarantees provided. Use or abuse on an as-is basis.

CLEAN HOUSE.
FLIRT AT BAR.
REPEAT.

One of the best hearing aids a man can have
is an attentive wife.
(Groucho Marx)

HOUSECLEANING AT 6 AM on a Saturday? Must tidy up. Must be a good provider. One might question who wears the pants in the family, but I don't. I have fully accepted that it's not me. All you should-have-been-ex-girlfriends-but-never-gave-me-the-time-of-day-when-I-approached-you-at-a-bar women eat your heart out. That's right. I do dishes. And windows. And clean the dryer's lint trap. Before *every* load.

Life isn't totally gender-reversed as I have a big night planned with the guys. Housework aside, I should try to log time with Deb. Balance out day with night. My queen-to-be awakes and makes her way to the couch. As she settles in, I approach. Like a tiger stalking its prey.

"Excuse me," a groggy Deb says.

"Doesn't the place look clean?" I offer.

"Not bad. Maybe you'll be a good husband after all. Now let's talk wedding."

Sadly, instead of picking off his innocent prey, this tiger has walked right into a steel-clawed trap and barely escapes. Quality time is officially over. I'm in the corner shaking like a sacrificial virgin at the mouth of a volcano. And the drums have just stopped.

Deb doesn't track the things most men are afraid their mates keep score of. Especially the "don't think about going out with *your* friends until we have *our* quality time" statistic (also known as the Time/Girl > Time/Boy Ratio). In fact, Deb's as easygoing as it gets. She backs my wacky endeavors 100 percent. I want to be a filmmaker; she buys me a camera. I want to be a Web master; she purchases my first domain. I want to be a couch potato; she brings home a PlayStation. Her compassion is one of the big reasons why I love her. But, we have a wedding to plan, so an actual trackless escape isn't an option at this moment.

"We should order heavier hors d'oeuvres. Don't you think?" Deb inquires.

Heavier? What does that mean? More expensive? More filling? Thicker toothpicks? How should I respond? "Why change a thing? Shouldn't we be coasting by now?" I offer.

"Oh, I'm coasting. But, you just seem to be doing a one-armed dog paddle up river."

Back to appetizers. "How about pigs in blankets? Who doesn't like them?"

"You either don't know me or don't love me. Or both."

For the most part, Deb has picked up my slack. Stuff seems to happen with or without my input. So is anything really lost in the process? Has the true storm yet to hit? Despite this (er, every) morning's bad start, Deb seems upbeat. Maybe it's that she's sitting on the warm towels I just took out of the dryer? Regardless, if she is happy, I am happy.

GUYS' NIGHT OUT. A mixed blessing at best. I enjoy our usual drinks, dinner, and more drinks routine but miss hitting on women. I still gawk, but what's the payoff? Before Deb, my attitude was "why not?" Even though I was never able to bed those hot chicks across the bar, I took comfort in knowing that a well-timed earthquake could toss one of them in my arms and, from that moment on, we would never look back.

Thanks to Deb, the thrill of the chase is no longer necessary. Bars have become more about chatting with friends. Of course, that assumes they want to chat with me. Some are still neck-deep in the chase and prefer the random "So, where do you work?" ice-breakers with a stranger than my deeper, more philosophical ruminations ("Am I crazy to get married?").

But this will eventually work out for the best. For all of us. Especially me. Legend has it that once I start wearing a wedding ring, plenty of women will longingly look at me as the one that got away. I'll feel vindicated. I'll feel superior. I'll rule the world. (Chances are, I'll still be the dork who believed his A-list party invitation was actually lost in the mail. At least I'll have someone by my side for reassurance.)

Are my thoughts the same as other guys due to be married? I could only guess, as I know no one to bounce my theories off of. Heaven forbid any of my friends get close to matrimony. I'm the lucky one. The trailblazer. The one with no one for real guidance.

Just to make sure, I survey my so-called support team:

Jake: the pretty one. Tall, dark, and handsome (or so I'm constantly told at bars by the women who keep falling for him and pushing me aside). A consummate bachelor, but still enjoys my company. I am too good of a wingman to let marriage get in his way. Jake's response: "Don't ask me."

Rick: Desperately seeking someone. Nice red-headed Irish boy. Wants to get married, but hasn't had a serious girlfriend in ten years. Always asking about the wedding, which is thoughtful, but tough to take sometimes. Rick's response: "Tell me everything."

Drew: the Teflon-coated relationship man. By all measures, he should be getting married along with me. Drew started dating his girlfriend a week after Deb and I met, but somehow has successfully sidestepped the M-word. When confronted with a premature (in his mind) "I love you," Drew was quick to answer with an "It's great women can express their feelings much better than men." Drew's response: "Keep Deb far away from my girlfriend."

Patrick: so close, yet so far from being married. Both big-hearted and big-stomached. My oldest friend, he knows me better than anyone. Patrick recently confided that he is going to marry his girlfriend. But not until he lands a job or starts receiving Social Security payments, whichever comes first. A tough call. The best thing about Patrick is that he knows me well enough to know not to bug me about the wedding. Patrick's response: "Have another beer."

I comfortably settle into an Amstel Light. Not the manliest drink, but right now my waistline is much more important than my penis size. But comfort doesn't last long. Rick bombards me with wedding questions.

"What time is the ceremony?"
"Have you picked out the tuxes?"
"Who am I going to be paired up with?"
"What kind of limo do we have?"
"You're serving pigs in blankets, right? Right?"

"Enough," I snort and venture to the other end of the bar. Even if it results in dreaded lone-man-at-bar-looking-desperate time.

But every cloud has a silver lining, and mine comes in the form of a conversation with two attractive women ordering a drink the same time I refill my beer (although now it's a manlier, gut-busting Bud). It's amazing what the misguided confidence (or fear) of getting married can bring out. That and my treating for their drinks.

But even if I want to keep my wedding a state (okay, world) secret, this conversation isn't about me. True to my pro-wingman form, I summon Rick over, forgiving his recent questioning. Tee him up for an easy in.

In truth, none of us are terrific openers or closers with women.

I prided myself on being the perfect filler: a semi-entertaining person who excels at the talking time between breaking the ice and shucking the clothes, both of which tend to be performed by someone else. I am merely holding someone's (read: usually Jake's) place, tiring the woman into a stupor.

Things go well the first few minutes. I am destined to hook Rick up. However, after a slight but healthy pause, Rick tries too hard to fill the void.

"So this guy is getting married soon. Isn't that great?"

Did Rick crack under the pressure? Just like the Titanic decades ago, Rick can't stop the sinking. In fact, he drills more holes in the hull.

"Yeah. I'm a groomsman. It's going to be so much fun. It's coming up soon. Yeah, fun. Great fun."

A kick in the groin would have been more fun. Rick's expression shows that he doesn't think much of his comment's consequences. He actually looks upset that I am not happier with the turn in conversation from the benefits of thongs with miniskirts to the choices of wedding songs for my big day. What was harmless flirtation now becomes the Spanish Inquisition, Part II.

"Is it a day or night wedding?"
"What color are the bridesmaid dresses?"
"How many groomsmen are there?"
"Where are you honeymooning?"
"You're not serving pigs in blankets, are you? Are you?"

Rick bows out, mid-bombardment. And after a few curt answers, I fall silent. Again, this tiger fails to capture his prey. Tail between my legs, I leave the women. But before returning to my pack, I am hugged from behind. Please be a female.

"Craig? How are you?"

Jessica. Never a girlfriend, despite previous attempts on my part. She looks gorgeous. But is it objective-to-the-casual-observer gorgeous? Or subjective-to-the-about-to-be-married-observer gorgeous? I haven't seen her for ages. Should I have tried harder way back when? Should I impress her now? Just to show

THE GUY'S GUIDE TO WEDDING RESPONSIBILITIES

Groom's key responsibilities

♠ Name names
- Prepare your side of the guest list.

♠ Go for the gold
- Choose the wedding bands, which can match or just have matching engravings.

♠ Keep it real
- Call the marriage license bureau to determine the necessary requirements and timing.
- Arrange for the blood test, if necessary.
- Schedule the marriage license appointment.

♠ Get from point A to B
- Drive to countless planning meetings.
- Book transportation to and from the ceremony and after the reception.

♠ Speak eloquently
- Give a toast at the rehearsal

Best man's key responsibilities

♠ Be a valet
- Serve as the groom's personal aide and adviser throughout the engagement and wedding.
- Help book accommodations for out-of-town groomsmen.

♠ Be a stylist
- Help with tux selection and other groomsmen's rentals.
- Decorate the getaway car with the bridal party.

♠ Be a pimp
- Plan the bachelor party. It shouldn't be hard to find help. What guy would turn down interviewing strippers, shopping for beer, and screening suitable pornography?

♠ Be there
- Attend the rehearsal dinner.
- Be announced with the maid of honor when the reception begins.

Groomsmen's key responsibilities

♠ Suit up
- Like the bridesmaids, you should pay for your wedding gear. Leave enough time for alterations.

♠ Party down
- Attend all pre-wedding festivities, including the engagement party, Couple's Shower, bachelor party, and rehearsal dinner. Two words: free grub.
- Help plan bachelor party.

♠ Gather around
- Usher guests to their seats. At traditional Christian ceremonies, guests of the bride's family sit on the left and guests of the groom's family sit on the right. At Jewish ceremonies, it's the opposite. With couples, take the woman's arm and escort her to a seat.

dinner in response to the best man's toast. Mention how lucky you are to marry your bride and thank your parents, in-laws, and guests.

Provide shelter
- Book a hotel room for your wedding night, unless you are leaving directly to the honeymoon.

Plan getaway
- Honeymoon getaway, that is. While you're probably going to pick a place with your bride, you are still responsible for most of the legwork.

- Dance with both the maid of honor and the bride during the first dance.

Be a pillar
- Stand next to the groom at the altar.
- Hold onto the bride's ring until the vows are exchanged.

Be a shepherd
- Corral the other groomsmen, making sure they're performing their wedding duties.
- Make sure everyone has fun at the wedding.

Be a conspirator
- Sign the marriage license along with the maid of honor.

Be a banker
- Hand the officiant his or her fee after the ceremony.
- Collect gift envelopes at the reception and possibly deposit into couple's bank account. No, you don't get to charge a handling fee.

Be a statesman
- Give the first toast at the reception, keeping it relatively clean.

- Be announced with the bridesmaid you escorted during the ceremony.
- Dance with bridesmaids and single female guests.

Help out
- Keep groom from running out the door.
- Answer questions.
- Make sure everyone has fun at the wedding.

Pitch in
- Purchase a wedding present by yourself or as a group gift with other groomsmen. Think big. And groom-friendly.

her that I'm still the cool, confident, and casual (three words no sane person would use to describe me right now) Craig she surely remembers? My mouth opens, preparing to utter something witty. At least something whimsical.

Jessica beats me to the punch. "I hear you're getting married. That's so great."

And what a punch. "And fun too. Don't forget about fun." Looking past Jessica, I spy Rick waving. Why do I get so worked up with people knowing about the wedding? I can't seem to hide it. And sooner or later, it will become public record. But does it have to be out there all the time? Certainly no one can blame me for trying to keep it quiet tonight. Well, no one except for Deb. And Rick.

DEB'S SOUND ASLEEP at home. She doesn't budge as I slip into bed. Strangely, I'm not satisfied by this.

"Guess who I ran into?" I ask.

No response.

"Yeah, she was cool. Haven't seen her in a while."

Still nothing.

"That Rick. What a character. We were talking with these girls."

Deb finally speaks. "I'm glad you're home, sweetheart. But, are you going to be the 'bitch' or what?"

"Bitch" is our loving term for bedroom spoonee. A role I gladly accept, as gender-bending as it sounds. So, silently, I roll over. Her arms wrap tightly around me. A perfect fit. I'm her bed bitch, the biggest huggable pillow on the market. She loves it. I love it. The world is back in order. At least for the next few hours.

IS THAT YOUR MINIVAN, MR. MICHAELS?

Marriage is a mistake every man should make.
(George Jessel)

DEB SNUGGLES UP around 6:30 AM. "Wake up," she says, perched on top of me.

Way too early for a sexual advance. There can only be one other reason for this disruption. Dutifully, I tend to my beloved. "Sorry. Snoring?"

"Worse," she offers.

"Drool?"

"Not even close." Her tone intensifies.

"Earthquake?" I try to sit up.

"You wish." Deb pins me down and lets out a series of rapid-fire questions that hit me like a jackhammer on concrete, but with much less success.

"Did we invite enough people?"
"Will any actually show up?"
"Aren't there any other cousins?"
"Why don't you have more friends?"

Not the best way to start God's day of rest. We head straight to the Web to check our RSVPs. Everything wedding related is kept online. Guest lists. Budgets. Events. Premade "sorry you can't make it to the wedding, but don't forget our registry" e-mails (my idea).

"Don't you want tons of people to cheer us on? Who else can we ask?" Deb pleads.

Think, Craig. Think. There's got to be a way out of this one. "Doesn't wedding etiquette dictate that it's too late to start asking more people?" I give myself props for citing Emily Post.

Mistake number one. Never bring up etiquette if you haven't helped in the last three months. I name names so fast that Senator McCarthy would have been proud to call me "son." Coworkers. Former coworkers. Faraway friends. Close-by acquaintances. The apartment manager. The pizza guy. It doesn't matter. I'm all about quantity, not quality.

With the A-, B-, and C-lists easily exhausted, we land somewhere near the J-list (merely one stop before the San Francisco White Pages). Still, I must produce more bodies. They even could be slightly chilled.

I really worry as Deb discusses economic theory.

"Let me put this in a way you business school graduates understand: we don't have enough guests to cover our fixed costs," Deb romantically reminds me. "A wedding is like an airline. At some point, it's better to have full seats than empty ones."

Milton Friedman would have been proud to call Deb "daughter."

EVENTUALLY HUNGER TRUMPS guest lists, but the cupboards are bare. Lately, Deb and I have been playing a simple game of Fill in the Blank. It's an adaptation of the old *Match Game* television game show. The one with Gene Rayburn hosting and questions like "The sheik said, 'Having one hundred wives is terrific! What's terrible is only having one BLANK.'"

In our home version, it's not as fun, there's no innocent sixties sex innuendos, and no door prizes. Deb would start off with:

"Who has time to BLANK when you have a wedding to plan? Maybe if you did anything you would understand."

This morning's BLANK is "grocery shopping."

"But Deb, you don't have a job," I say.

Mistake number two. Off to the grocery store we go. Normally, grocery shopping is my responsibility, even though I hate going by myself. I always wind up bumping into countless couples roaming the aisles hand in hand, checking their lists, planning fun dinner parties, simultaneously comparing steak expiration dates, and stealing kisses near the frozen meats. My meats are frozen too; where are my kisses?

But today, Deb wants to be close by. Guess she wants to keep me from making a third mistake, like returning home with a package of Oreo Double Stufs, which Deb hates but was my last girlfriend's favorite snack. I had to eat the whole package in one sitting to prove that it was me who really loved them. Some punishment, huh?

I am on a Safeway Club Card tear. I'd eat the same type of apple for weeks if it were half price. Today it's Fuji apples. Deb thinks I lack variety. I have variety. Over the long run.

Deb's still preoccupied with finding more guests. Is that her voice on the PA system?

"We have a potential invite on aisle six."

Our shopping cart looks like the Korean demilitarized zone. Lots of food tensions and incompatibilities. Did I know Deb eats Special K? Does she know I like chocolate-covered Gummy Bears? We loiter in very different aisles. She loves salt. I love sugar. She loves jerky. I love licorice. She loves fish. I love beef. Is this healthy? Can we ever truly buy in bulk? Which genes will our kids inherit? If their genes come from Deb, I'd say graceful ones. If their genes come from me, I'd say husky. And corduroy. And not the cool cords, either.

We save over 30 percent today. A new record. How exciting. Does Donna, our checkout clerk, pick up on the fact that my joy from securing two dozen eggs for the price of one is merely masking a recent sexual dry spell?

"You see. It doesn't take much to save. Look at the receipt. Not bad, huh?" I ask.

Am I unwittingly moving toward a minivan purchase? Am I being actively domesticated against my will? I never balanced a checkbook before, and now I'm counting pennies, thinking about college funds, and loading up on gallons of ketchup. Store brand to boot. I cannot afford to splurge on Heinz anymore. Generic all the way!

✧

WE SPEND THE rest of the day on the couch in silence trying to make a dent in the groceries. I check the Web to see if the new *Survivor* contestants have been picked. Damn it. It should have been me. I made it to the semifinals. Mostly due to my brilliant application I sent a few months after getting engaged. Deb even helped me with the answers. Anything for a laugh. And a million dollars.

"What is your primary motivation for being on the show?" the questionnaire asked.

> "To avoid getting married. At least for another year. Competing on *Survivor* is the only (happy) way for me to get out of my wedding. While I love my fiancée, the marriage process has taken its toll on my manhood. *Survivor* would be the ultimate recharge for my Y chromosome. I know, a weekend in Vegas might do the trick, but I think *Survivor* will offer me better odds than any craps table or strip joint. Besides, I am getting married in Vegas and don't want to desecrate that town any more than necessary before our upcoming nuptials."

My video was even better. Three straight minutes of me trying to escape the wedding. I begged for a reprieve. A chance to survive.

The day after I FedExed my application, *Survivor* called and said they were coming to San Francisco to interview me. They also had some additional questions.

"You're Jewish, right?"

"Why?"

"Is Deb Jewish?"

"No."

"Perfect. Are you physically fit?"

"Fit?"

"In shape. We couldn't tell much from the video. You were mostly sitting down."

"Of course. I run marathons in my sleep. No worries."

The phone didn't fully rest on its cradle before I dialed my gym, a place I frequent as often as I change the batteries in our smoke detector. Within minutes, I had booked a trainer every night that week.

Julio, a three-time Cuban boxing champ, put me to work. He made me wear a Neoprene band around my midsection to promote sweating. Some might call it a girdle. But, to me, it's a body enhancement device. The workouts weren't fun, but a month later I was a new man. At least one who from an upright position could see more than his big toe.

For the in-person *Survivor* interview, I wore a shirt one size smaller than usual, to show off my new physique. I thought about donning the girdle, but was afraid they might ask me to undress. The interview lasted a half-hour. Even with repeated flexing and posing, they still asked if I were fit.

In the end, I was told I wasn't "confrontational enough for *Survivor*." I can't argue with that these days. Especially since wedding planning has perfected my compromising skills. Or are they submissive skills? Oh well, there goes my last chance for an acceptable escape. And a way to pocket a million dollars. Wedding, here I come. Financial ruin, I'm already there.

Deb suggests I break out the girdle again. For our picture's sake.

THE GUEST LIST:
KEEPING UP WITH THE JONESES

THE TYPICAL NUMBER of guests invited to a wedding is one hundred and sixty-four. Please don't take it too personally if Aunt Martha bails. On average, 20 percent of your guests won't attend. And to keep things orderly, you should have one usher per forty guests.

Does your guest list feel like the Chicago phonebook? Here are a few cutting tips:

- **Workmates.** Limit the office party to the barest of essentials: your boss and your assistant.
- **Distant relatives.** You never see them anyway, so why start now?
- **Kids.** Arrange baby-sitting services at the hotels or, better yet, hope guests leave the rugrats at home. Set a minimum age, and don't make any exceptions.
- **Quid pro quos.** Just because you were invited to their wedding doesn't mean you have to invite them to yours. But don't be an elitist, especially if you are inviting mutual friends.
- **Dates.** Limit guest extras to only husbands, wives, and fiancés. Although, you should allow your wedding party to bring dates, even if they just met at the tuxedo shop.

■

WHAT A TYPICAL WEDDING INVITATION SHOULD SAY:

(Name of your fiancée's parents)
request the honor of your presence
at the marriage of their daughter
(Name of your fiancée)
to
(Your name)
on
(Day of the week), the (Day of month)
of (Month)
at (Time, spelled out) o'clock
(Place: name and address of reception location)

IF YOU ARE PAYING FOR THE WEDDING, YOU DON'T HAVE TO INCLUDE PARENTS:

(Name of your fiancée)
and
(Your name)
request the honor of your presence at their marriage
on
(Day of the week), the (Day of month)
of *(Month)*
at *(Time, spelled out)* o'clock
(Place: name and address of reception location)

You can also include your parents' names as well. This depends on whether all your parents are still alive, who is paying for the wedding, or religious traditions.

THEN THERE'S ALWAYS WHAT HER PARENTS PROBABLY WANT TO SAY:

(Name of your fiancée's parents)
Request the honor of your (cash) presents at the marriage
of their daughter
(Name of your fiancée)
to
(Your name),
whom we hope soon takes a step up the corporate ladder and moves out of the mail room, or at least out of our basement
on
(Day of the week), the (Day of month)
of *(Month)*
at *(Time, spelled out)* o'clock
(Place: name and address of reception location)

BODY PAINTING,
ONE-TENTH SCALE.

The secret of a happy marriage remains a secret.
(Henny Youngman)

THANK GOD IT'S Monday. I never thought I would be this eager for the workweek to begin, especially with the Sunday night butterflies I've suffered since kindergarten. How will I survive wedding eve? A late-night call to Mom for PB&J sandwiches, crusts off, and cut in triangles? With a juice box chaser?

According to Craig's Fourth Law of Thermo-wed-dynamics (my latest in-bed neurotic hypothesis), one's wedding pressure is inversely proportional to the square of the distance between fiancés. I must leave the house soon, lest I implode. If only my company had a branch in the Czech Republic.

One day, this law along with my other three will serve as the underlying theory describing not just a man's engagement, but all men / women interactions. I predict a Nobel Prize in twenty years. Or at least be chosen as *Maxim*'s Man of the Year (except for the physique part).

Craig's First Law: For every wedding to-do, there's an equal and opposite groom hoping not to get caught not doing it.

Craig's Second Law: A guest list will continue to build until it fills the container the wedding will be held in.

Craig's Third Law: Wedding equilibrium only exists in the millisecond between his "I do" and her "I do." At any other time, one's life is in a complete state of entropy. Get used to it.

ON THE TRAIN ride to work. I become dizzy from the bumps and blurs looking out the window. House after house passes by. Each probably filled with happy, married people. Couples who successfully planned their wedding somehow, some way. Men, confident in their abilities, venturing forth each day to conquer the world. Why not me? Maybe they don't have as much time to be introspective. After all, the roar of a train in front of their houses every twelve minutes must take its toll on their sanity. Note to self: research real estate close to San Francisco International Airport's Runway Two. That should be loud enough for a blissful life. Until then, I must get it together.

I'm committed to wedding stuff the entire morning. It's not that hard, and thanks to Deb, I have copies of today's to-do list taped to everything. I only hope the crunch in my pants is just another copy, or else I'm going to have a bigger worry this morning than calling the videographer.

My eyes refocus, revealing my reflection in the window. I can do it. I am ready. Willing. Able. I feel good. I feel like a groom. I even call Deb.

"Nothing stopping me today, baby," I declare.

"Go dog. Go," Deb cheers back.

That's right, nothing's stopping me. Until I trip over a pile of boxes in my office, landing at the feet of my new officemate. If I ever needed an excuse to procrastinate, Nico looks like he'll fit the bill. I don't remember interviewing him, but Nico swears my "this is a ten billion dollar company in two years, guaranteed" pitch sealed the deal. Was I that persuasive with Deb? Is she expecting a meteoric rise out of me as well?

A lanky, out-there chap from Holland, Nico is one of those guys who has never been close to getting married, let alone a serious girlfriend. Not the positive influence I need. Too "ready, willing, and able to pounce on the American female" (his words, not mine) to be bothered with relationships.

Nico whiteboards his soon-to-be net worth from our stock options. "IPO, next year?" Nico gleefully asks.

I play along. "Sure."

"We're going to be loaded. So why are you messing that up by getting married?"

"It's the right thing to do."

"Pregnant?"

"No!" As it turns out, wedding planning is the ultimate contraceptive.

"Rich?"

"No."

"Well she sounds lovely. Good for you mate."

I decide to wait a day before inviting Nico to the wedding.

✧

As I stare at a PowerPoint slide ("Product Roadmap version 36: This time it's for real"), Nico spends his morning instant messaging, talking about this chick and that chick, this party and that party, this trip and that trip. I keep reminding myself that looks can be deceiving and the grass isn't always greener. But it would be fun to play in someone else's yard for a day or two.

Deb calls for a friendly check on how things are going.

I lie. "Working on the honeymoon."

"Really?" She sounds pleased.

I feel dirty.

✧

Deb's expecting an exotic locale, like Bali or Thailand, which to my family translates into Terroristville. I'd be happy with a five-day SuperSaver pass at Disneyland and maybe a few movie studio tours, but somehow I don't think that's most females' dream honeymoon. Well, most females over eight.

I switch between the Lonely Planet and the State Department's Travel Advisory Web sites. With the occasional Center for Disease Control cross-reference. Where to go? Where to go?

My family suggested a cross-country RV trip. That could be fun. Yosemite, Mount Rushmore, Skyline Drive. Even a swing through Disney World. (If we're driving, why not go the extra twenty-five hundred miles for EPCOT, right?) I'll be in the captain's chair. Deb can be the lookout for bearmobiles (CB talk for police cars) and turn twenties (exit ramps). We would talk, laugh, eats bags and bags of potato chips, and hit every Waffle House, IHOP, In-N-Out, Cracker Barrel, and Denny's along the way. When someone calls to talk, we'll tell them we're 10-6 (busy) with 10-17 (urgent business). It is our honeymoon, after all. We'll collect friends, thimbles, and magnets from every state.

Deb was briefed on that part. I managed to keep my parents' "and we could join you every now and then" comment from her. That's probably not the best way to indoctrinate Deb into the Michaels way of life, love, and visitation.

Deb's family isn't too worried about our travels. Deb traveled to Africa, Israel, South America, and all of Europe by herself. Me? I wasn't allowed to take a bus to the mall until a year after I started to shave daily.

"*Ik kan niet geloven hoe* pussy whipped *mijn collega is,*" Nico says into his phone.

How nice of him to mention me to his folks.

"What else are you doing today?" Deb asks.

"Stuff. Don't worry."

"Tell me."

"Not in front of Nico."

"Who?"

Quietly, "My new officemate."

Loudly, "Oh, did you invite him yet?"

As I shut down for the day (that is, shut down my work computer; my wedding system is just warming up and it has one helluva battery life), Drew calls.

"A pottery shop? Aren't you getting enough breakables as gifts?" Drew inquires.

"We're going to paint our own wedding cake topper."

"Why?"

"Love."

"Again. Why?"

"It's cheaper. Maybe fun. Definitely cheaper."

Like trips to the grocery store, I have spied happy couples smiling, painting, and holding hands at our local pottery place. Why not us? And why start with something simple and meaningless, like a coffee mug? I don't do things half-assed. It's all-assed.

"The cake topper is the ultimate symbol of us," Deb reminds me. "It must convey our passion and commitment. Everyone will see it. It will be in our pictures, videos, and memories forever."

"And save us fifty dollars."

"Hmmm."

"It'll be straight from our heart."

"Grrr."

Have I taken the Vegas theme too far with my painting? Deb gets a purple dress. I'm now wearing a bright green jacket, navy pants, navy and yellow shirt. Her hair is suddenly black, mine blond.

"Wait until it dries, sweetheart. Don't cry. It just needs to be baked and shellacked." I wish I could get baked and shellacked. "Worst case, trailer-park cute."

"Trailer-park cute?"

Oops. When Deb tells people that she's getting married in Vegas, it screams trashy. She switched to saying Henderson, the correct town (twenty miles east of Las Vegas). But when people ask where Henderson is located, we get the "ah, too-cheap-for-Vegas" look.

In five days, we'll see the topper masterpiece which will still give me enough time to FedEx a more traditional one directly to Vegas (er, Henderson).

There are no more tears when Deb comes back from washing up. Newfound optimism? Newfound trust? Newfound shellac sniffing?

HERE COMES THE BRIDE.
HERE COMES THE GROOM.
THERE GOES $26,173.

2005 AVERAGE WEDDING costs

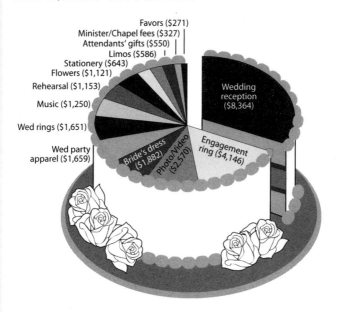

Favors ($271)
Minister/Chapel fees ($327)
Attendants' gifts ($550)
Limos ($586)
Stationery ($643)
Flowers ($1,121)
Rehearsal ($1,153)
Music ($1,250)
Wed rings ($1,651)
Wed party apparel ($1,659)
Bride's dress ($1,882)
Photo/Video ($2,570)
Engagement ring ($4,146)
Wedding reception ($8,364)

Watch your pennies (or C-notes)!

Forty-five percent of couples spend more on the wedding than they planned.

Source: 2005 American Wedding Study, The Fairchild Bridal Group

WHO PAYS WHAT?

SPECIFIC FINANCIAL RESPONSIBILITIES

Bride's family

Wedding planner

Invitations and announcements

Bride's gown, accessories, and
   hair/makeup

Transportation for the wedding party
   from the ceremony to the reception

All floral arrangements and
   boutonnieres and corsages for bride's
   family and bridesmaids

Photography and videography

Music

Wedding reception

Bride

Groom's wedding ring

Gift for groom

Gifts for bridesmaids

Groom's family

Rehearsal dinner

Groom

Marriage license

Officiant's fee

Bride's bouquet

Boutonnieres and corsages for groom's
   family and groomsmen

Bride's engagement and wedding rings

Gifts for groomsmen

Gift for bride

Tuxedo

Honeymoon

PINCHING PENNIES WITHOUT PITCHING FITS

ARE WEDDING COSTS spiraling out of control?

Have you considered donating blood as a second income? Maybe even an organ or two?

Hold on. All's not lost. There are some ways to cut corners without you having to cut out a kidney. But like any surgical procedure, proceed with caution. It's one thing to not do anything for your wedding. But it's another to not do anything and attempt to cheapen the affair.

Plan ahead. While this goes against everything a man stands for, you'll save money by booking things early. Besides avoiding rush charges, you can also avoid any bidding wars over the "must-have" chef/photographer/florist/you-name-it.

Embrace technology. It's the Internet Age, so go online to find vendors. You'll be surprised to find what's getting outsourced these days. Besides getting favors drop shipped direct from China, you should take advantage of the tools right under your nose, like laser printers, digital cameras, CD burners, and e-mail.

Go all-in. In-clusive, that is. Many venues offer package deals that include services you would normally have to secure elsewhere, like catering. They might also provide day-of wedding planner support to make sure all goes well on your big day.

Start early. Whether it's earlier in the day, earlier in the week, or earlier in the season, you might save a bundle by avoiding the sought-after Saturday-night time slot.

Mix and match. While imported foods, premium-shelf alcohol, and world-famous pastries might impress your guests, you don't have to pay top dollar for everything. Pick a few lower-cost appetizers, consider hosting a buffet, serve only wine and beer during dinner, limit alcohol to custom cocktails (e.g., martinis and cosmos), and, if you invite enough people, have two cakes (a fancy one for showing and eating, and a plain one for just eating).

Call time-outs. Limit the photographer and/or videographer's schedule. Just make sure the shots you want occur during the actual filming time. Although can anyone really know when a conga line will form?

Pool resources. If people you know are getting married around your wedding day, try sharing some costs, recycling decorations, and obtaining volume discounts. Even if you don't know anyone, see if the reception venue can assist in reusing some supplies.

Do it yourself. Break out the warehouse club card and bring your own alcohol. Apply summer-camp arts-and-crafts skills and make your own party favors. Go to work early and use your company's printer. Wait until dark and clip your own roses. And forget it just being DIY. Recruit, draft, and beg your friends for assistance. Okay, her friends.

Stand firm. Try to negotiate discounts or extra services with your vendors. Also, make sure you review each contract's fine print to avoid additional charges. And, wherever possible, don't tell places it's for a wedding. That little fact might avoid any "we got you by your shorts" pricing.

Go off the beaten path. You might be able to lower your expenses dramatically by picking an out-of-the-way place for your reception. It might even be worth checking out just the surrounding towns. Be sure to strike the right balance between saving money and costing your guests more to get to the wedding. And if you find a real bargain site, keep telling her "it's rustic, not run-down."

Adopt a less-is-more attitude. When possible, pick the simpler decorations, choose less labor-intensive foods and flowers, minimize the band, and reduce the guest list. Besides saving you money, it'll probably save you time and anxiety in the long run.

Elope. The granddaddy of cost cutting. And if you play your cards right, you might still get some presents. Especially if you throw a casual post-elopement party for your friends and family.

REVENGE OF THE PROM TUX.

A successful man is one who makes more money
than his wife can spend.
A successful woman is one who can find such a man.
(Lana Turner)

WE CAN'T SEEM to go a day without spending five hundred dollars. First on today's spend list is wedding favors. Deb takes it all in stride. "All this will happen once. Twice at most," she promises.

"Just make sure you stick it to the next guy as well."

Her dedication is amazing. Triathletes don't have this much endurance. What would happen if more preparations were left to me? Since my pre-Deb world consisted of a futon; twelve plastic tubs filled with videotapes of *Alf, Melrose Place,* and *The Simpsons;* and three TVs, I'd probably be serving turkey sandwiches on decorative paper towels. But now that my coupled life includes Deb's leather couch, wood tables, metallic silverware, and multidrawer dressers, expectations are much higher. Even if it's Vegas.

GETTING MARRIED IN Las Vegas has its challenges. We thought about swapping the traditional husband-and-wife kiss for a his-and-hers pull on the *Wheel of Fortune* slot machine. (I asked. Deb denied.) Rabbi Elvis (a young Elvis, never an old one) could perform the ceremony. (I begged. Deb punched.) Or at least Elvis could make change for the guests. (I joked. Deb considered.)

We also could host an event so bland, it would feel like any other banquet hall wedding, complete with those lovely movable walls that easily adjust to our exact party size.

But no. This is Vegas. I desire more than a windowless room, carpeted walls, and a sign ensuring that the Halloran-Michaels wedding guests would not accidentally wander into Tom Shank's retirement party or Rachel Stein's Bat Mitzvah. While I don't contribute much to the planning process, I certainly want to bask in the party's glory. But I need not worry. Deb is planning an awesome wedding.

And she just found awesome party favors, too. Fun, sinful, and right on the money. As long as you are dealt twenty-one. With a few double-clicks and a double-check of my credit balance, we order four hundred decks of Deb & Craig playing cards, more than triple our guest list.

"Isn't that a bit excessive?" I try to cut the order down a notch.

"Don't you want our twenty grandkids to have them to play with while watching our wedding video?" Deb argues.

There's only one answer to that question. "Of course, dear. You're right."

And truth be told, she is. Why shouldn't we be the crazy, fun branch of our family tree that will be admired for generations. "Is that all for now?" I ask.

"Not even close. We've got music, seating, linens, flowers, tuxedos . . ."

✧

TUXEDOS. TIME TO pick, fit, and pray. You won't see me on the cover of *GQ* any time soon, but I've had a few memorable moments in formalwear history. Okay, maybe one: junior prom. All-white. Tails and top hat, too. With a powder blue cummerbund and tie to match my date's dress.

Besides our matching attire, we were such the mismatched duo. She was short, I was tall. She liked malls, I liked *Missile Command*. She liked dancing, I liked Dungeons & Dragons. She had lots of friends, I had . . . her. But, we still made a "handsome couple," according to our parents, who hosted a joint prom send-off party. Complete with distant relatives, flash photography, and the standard Dad-to-limo-driver safety lecture. ("Hands always at ten and two o'clock, got it?")

I tried my best to impress her by Walking Like an Egyptian, whispering that I can't live With or Without You, and trying hard to Fight for My Right to Party. But I didn't get far in that battle. Prom night consisted of a half-hour of making out and an over-that-powder-blue-puffy-dress breast feel before we both passed out on the floor of a friend's house.

AT MR. TUX, Deb couldn't have been more supportive.

"Pick whatever you want, sweetheart. It's up to you."

Ninety-eight percent of the time, any man would kill to hear such support from his woman. But not now. "What about this?" I tug at the waist, pleading for help.

"If you like it, I like it."

"That doesn't help."

"See how I feel?" Deb snorts.

"Touché," I scream out as Deb leaves for the food court.

"Yeah, it's a little tight in the rear. But we can let it out," Jason, my certified tailor, says.

Thank you, Mr. Tux guy.

Being loved is a great thing. But it's not helping much right now. I'm stuck with Jason, a seventeen-year-old "expert" tuxedo salesperson, who is having a tough time staying off his cell phone, let alone tending to my physiological needs. Where are all the cute Gap girls, telling you that you look great in whatever they are trying to push that week, when you need them?

Consciously or subconsciously, I forgot a white dress shirt to try on with the tux. And Mr. Tux won't let me borrow one.

I improvise and tape a sheet of white paper to my chest,

complete with a Sharpie bowtie. Voilà. Even Jason takes notice. Or is it exception?

"Day or night?" Jason asks.

"Day, then night," I respond.

"Traditional or contemporary?"

"Contemporary, with some tradition."

"Vest or cummerbund? Point collar or pique? Long tie or bow? Wing tip or square toe?"

"Enough." I need some air. And an Orange Julius. And a hot dog on a stick.

When I return, I decide to take charge ("Finally," Jason declares). The last time I had formal pictures taken was in high school. I've got better hair, teeth, and skin now. And a great woman by my side. Time to take advantage of the situation.

An hour and three Sharpies later, we agree (one vote for Deb, one for me, and of course one for Jason, who argues that, as my certified tuxedo expert, he gets two votes and veto power) to a three-button jacket, straight tie, and silver-gray vest.

The cool thing about being the groom is that my tuxedo is free. Finally, a much-needed improvement in my financial outlook. Then Deb reminds me that we're buying all her bridesmaids' dresses. Oh. Back to a bear market.

SUIT UP!

DID YOU THINK a black tie is as stuffy as it gets? Think again. White ties (along with a black tailcoat) define a formal evening wedding. But now the semiformal tuxedo, with its black dinner jacket and tie, is the more popular choice.

If you are a stickler for formality and having a day wedding, wear a morning suit. This consists of a gray or black cutaway coat, gray vest, striped trousers, and a four-in-hand tie or ascot. Not that traditional? Wear a black or gray short jacket, called a stroller, instead of the cutaway.

And if you don't want the bride to be the only one in white, push for a summer or hot-climate wedding so you can don a white jacket. Just be easy on the lace. And don't pull up the sleeves like Crockett and Tubbs.

If things get ugly with your fiancée, just toss this zinger out there:

What's black and white and red all over?
A bloody groom if his tux doesn't fit.

If she laughs, then you know she's the one. If she doesn't, that's okay. You'll just know that this author's not her type.

■

IS THAT A RULER IN YOUR POCKET, OR ARE YOU JUST HAPPY TO GET SIZED?

KEY BODY MEASUREMENTS for your tuxedo include:

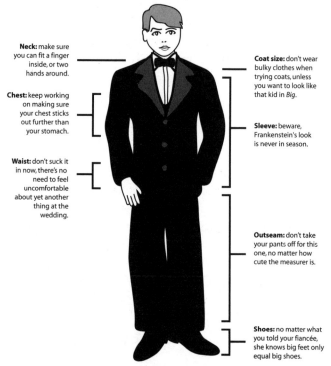

Neck: make sure you can fit a finger inside, or two hands around.

Chest: keep working on making sure your chest sticks out further than your stomach.

Waist: don't suck it in now, there's no need to feel uncomfortable about yet another thing at the wedding.

Coat size: don't wear bulky clothes when trying coats, unless you want to look like that kid in *Big*.

Sleeve: beware, Frankenstein's look is never in season.

Outseam: don't take your pants off for this one, no matter how cute the measurer is.

Shoes: no matter what you told your fiancée, she knows big feet only equal big shoes.

TIE TIED?

HERE'S A HANDY guide to tying a bowtie:

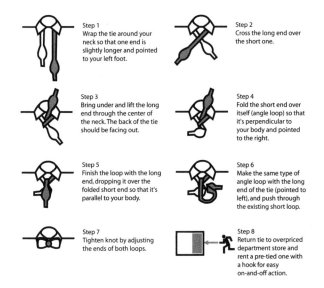

Step 1
Wrap the tie around your neck so that one end is slightly longer and pointed to your left foot.

Step 2
Cross the long end over the short one.

Step 3
Bring under and lift the long end through the center of the neck. The back of the tie should be facing out.

Step 4
Fold the short end over itself (angle loop) so that it's perpendicular to your body and pointed to the right.

Step 5
Finish the loop with the long end, dropping it over the folded short end so that it's parallel to your body.

Step 6
Make the same type of angle loop with the long end of the tie (pointed to left), and push through the existing short loop.

Step 7
Tighten knot by adjusting the ends of both loops.

Step 8
Return tie to overpriced department store and rent a pre-tied one with a hook for easy on-and-off action.

■

GIFTS FOR YOUR GROOMSMEN: SHOW YOUR POSSE THAT YOU CARE.

YOU SHOULD GIVE a gift to your groomsmen to thank them for being a part of the wedding, being there for all those years, and being a good alibi in case the bachelor party goes bad (or good). Typically, the gift is delivered during the rehearsal.

Some gifts to consider for your groomsmen:

Swiss army knife	Sunglasses
Ski lift tickets	Cufflinks
Round of golf	Money clip
DVD of favorite movie	CD of favorite music
Toolkit	Custom bowling shirt

Travel kit	Massage certificate
Sport tickets	Comedy tickets
Concert tickets	Barware
Beer-of-the-month club	Engraved flask
Bottle of wine or liquor	Watch

■

WHILE YOU'RE AT it, here are some gift ideas for your bride. Get used to it.

We know. You gave her the ring. You gave her your heart. You're giving her all that special attention. Why a gift for being your bride? Because. That's all you need to know. And commit to memory. Actually, she's done a lot to make your wedding a memorable event. Probably more than you. Give her something to show your appreciation and love during the rehearsal or on your wedding day (just make sure someone else gives it to her if it's before the wedding—no peeking).

Spa certificate

Jewelry

Perfume

Charm bracelet

Framed photo of a fun event you shared

Poem from your heart

Story of a favorite moment with her

Family heirloom

Something from her favorite author, painter, etc.

Honeymoon item

LITTLE BLUE BOX.
BIG-ASS BILL.

Men who have a pierced ear are better prepared for marriage.
They've experienced pain and bought jewelry.
(Rita Rudner)

HUMP DAY. NOT the good kind. Like the kind when you're first dating and everything is new and exciting. You play connect-the-dots with your girlfriend's freckles, tracing major star constellations. You stay in bed all day and night, feasting on each other. You watch porn without feeling ashamed because, for once, you're with someone (a female someone).

Today's just a plain Wednesday. No body art. No ravishing. No porn fest. But there is one bit of excitement today: we get to pick our wedding bands. "The proverbial handcuffs," according to Nico. Am I really ready to join the ball-and-chain gang? Be branded for life? Don a platinum M for all to see?

No time to think. Work beckons. After all, I have precious metal to pay for. And it's selling for almost a thousand dollars an ounce on the Chicago Board of Trade, so I best not be late.

"Tiffanies? That's going to set you back," Rick says, half-concerned, half-gloating. With him being girlfriendless for the better part of this year, he's been able to buy a new car, go to Fiji for two weeks, and save up for a rainy day. With me being girlfriended for the better part of my life, I've been able to drive a beater car, go to Florida with my folks (Disney family reunion, or as I like to say, "It's really a small, small world when you can't ditch a family trip at thirty years old"), and save up for a misty morning. As long as that morning occurs in 2019. Late 2019.

"It's Tiffany. As in *Breakfast at Tiffany's,*" I reply (a classic movie that any man trying to impress any woman should know. Put that alongside *An Affair to Remember* on your DVD rack at home, and it's instant point-scoring with a date).

"Don't you mean *Bankrupt at Tiffany's?*" Rick's now full-gloating.

"No diamond. No worries," I offer. And pray. Pray that I don't get taken to the cleaners like I almost did with the engagement ring. Because what do I know about jewelry?

✧

JEWELRY IS AS foreign to me as my being invited to a ménage-a-trois. I had come to terms with having just ménage-a-deux, which by itself was a step up from my mostly ménage-a-un-hand existence in high school and most of college. I just keep reminding myself what I've heard: it's not that great, and you get very jealous afterward. But, like anyone with a Y chromosome, I wonder. And dream.

The only piece of jewelry I have ever worn was a fourteen-carat gold or gold-painted (I can't remember. No, I don't want to remember.) bracelet. A gift from my junior prom girlfriend, she of the baby-blue-matching-my-cummerbund-with-blinding-white-tux dress. Back in Massapequa, Long Island, gold bracelets were all the rage. Usually, Italian guys were the ones decked out in gold. They also dated hot chicks and drove IROC-Zs. I didn't want the gold or cars, just the girls. But those things always seem to come in threes and I, the Jew with part-time access to my mom's Buick, didn't get the hot girls. Just a nice, prudish one from Levittown. While her gift was sincere, I only wore it when she was around. It didn't feel right dangling on my wrist and getting caught on my argyle sweaters. The Italian guys didn't wear argyle, either. Maybe that was my real problem?

✧

MY ONLY SENSE of relief in today's ring shopping adventure was The Rock already on Deb's hand. Thank God for The Rock. If there was one piece of advice I would give any guy, it would be to supersize your diamond as best as you can. Actually, do it better than you can. Bump it up by at least half a carat. I realize that this might be easier said than done, but do it. And don't even think about buying cubic zirconia. I read in *Men's Health* that one in eleven men would buy CZ if they could get away with it. Trust me, you won't. It might not be today, tomorrow, or next week, but someday you'll get ratted out. And there won't be enough real diamonds (or diamond-tipped diamonds) to dig your way out of that hole.

I was lucky. Our family had a friend that ultimately saved the day. But before that family connection was secured, granting me a prize worth more than a golden ticket from Willy Wonka, I waded through the fiery, hellish waters of diamond retailing. Fortunately, I was only scorched a bit from my three store visits.

Store Number One: I tried to pull the "But I'm a tribe member, too" Jewish discount card. No dice. I might have jumped into the deep end too soon. The salesman showed me a ton of diamonds. One by one, they each looked like the perfect diamond. But, alas, there is no perfect diamond. Not in my price range, that is. Juggling the Four Cs on the spot (because like cars, they don't want you to leave without buying) was worse than any multivariate calculus problem I—or Albert Einstein—had ever faced. Net net: I ran out of the place.

Store Number Two: I put my game face on and visited the place where I "always have a friend in the business." Armed with a three-ring binder full of Internet research (did you know the average person pays twice what they should for an engagement ring, and the average diamond has been over-graded by two grades to enhance its salability and weighed incorrectly to increase the jeweler's profit margin?), I haggled, screamed, and even accused my new friend of "having his thumb on the scale." Net net: They ran me out of the place.

Store Number Three: the worst. The saleswoman was hot. So hot, the store crossed the line. It's okay for a saleswoman to be hot enough to lull me into taking her advice. And losing control of my wallet. But she shouldn't be too hot for me to forget who I'm buying the ring for. Or what my name is. Net net: We chatted for two hours, but ultimately she didn't believe my "I'm doing research for a book" line.

I was about to try Store Number Four in Chinatown, but mercifully, I was called up to the big leagues. Diamond District, New York City. The high-rise offices in midtown Manhattan weren't what I expected (I had grand visions of jewel-encrusted elevator buttons, leading into gold-adorned palatial rooms—just think anything Trump), but my business with Jeff, our family connection, was pleasantly surprising. As pleasant as a frontal lobotomy. And as surprising as a colonoscopy. I merely said "do what you think is best" and put my fate in Jeff's hands.

Having an inkling of a retirement fund already in the bank paid off. And in one fell swoop, it also paid out. Two and sixteen-hundredth carats, or, as I like to say, just a hair over two and a half Cs. Bling bling. Or at least, bling.

After the fact, I realized that this is indeed a foolproof engagement ring purchase plan:

Step 1: Identify a female for support, knowledge, and taste. Not your mom. Not your fiancée's mom. Not any mom. If she knows your girlfriend, make sure she can keep a secret. If she doesn't, enter stores from the rear. No need for your fiancée-to-be to catch you in a compromising position without any benefit of being compromised.

Step 2: Find someone who knows someone who knows something about diamonds. Lie, beg, cheat, or steal in order to find that person. This is your Sherpa. Your North Star. Your "Never Pay Retail, You Idiot" Sage. I will forever be in debt (figuratively and for at least another three years, literally) to Jeff.

Step 3: Tell your appointed diamond expert how much you want to spend.

Step 4: Dig deeper and add at least a zero to your budget once your expert stops laughing.

Step 5: Whenever asked by anyone not wearing a magnifying glass in their eye or a diamond so big it rivals the sun, round up your diamond's carat weight as much as you can without your bride-to-be or her friends calling bullshit. Sorry, no formula here. It's an imperfect science at best.

DEB IS WAITING for me in front of Tiffany & Co., a.k.a. Mecca for every bride-to-be. Apparently, Tiffany is the only store that has a band to match my (well, Jeff's) "exquisite taste in engagement rings." Goody for me.

Here's another jewelry tip: know the difference between Tiffany's front and back sections (although in some stores, the sections are differentiated by floors). In the front section, you will shell out lots of money for sparkly, heavy, stunning things. In the back section, you can get nice, cute gifts and still make your car payment. I have ventured into the back section a few times, never making eye contact with those upper-crust folks (customers and salespeople alike) in the front. It takes patience and lots of assistance, but one can find inexpensive presents that look great in Tiffany's signature blue box. Granted, these are gifts more appropriate for a sixteen-year-old who got straight As for the first time, but a blue box is a blue box is a blue box. One day, I would graduate to the front. Fortunately, it wasn't for the engagement ring. That would have probably tripled my cost. Shopping frontward to buy Deb's wedding band seems like a good transitional step. Maybe not good, but reasonable. Maybe not reasonable, but tolerable. Maybe not tolerable, either. But that's a fight for another day.

Deb knows exactly what she wants at Tiffany's. I even think she and Valerie, our chipper and, thank goodness, not too hot saleswoman, share a "hey girlfriend" nod as we approach. Strolling between the glass cabinets, ones that store more than a thousand times my earnings potential, I stay vigilant and keep one eye on the closest exit. Even when it may be behind me. It doesn't really matter. Three seconds and almost a grand later, we order Deb's ring. Too quick to hurt. But our shopping spree isn't over yet. While I dare not object to the cost of Deb's band, my eyes, wallet, and butt clench in anticipation of what's in store for me.

With Deb done, it's my turn to get sized, shaped, and swindled. Ninety-nine percent of the past decade—and hopefully the next decade or two—my size has been simple: extra-large tall shirts and thirty-six by thirty-six pants. Ring size? No clue. "Never knew, never wanted to know" is what I professed to many of my girlfriends. After they were sound asleep, of course. And after yelling their names at the top of my lungs first to make sure they were sound asleep. And doing so from the all-night diner across the street.

But finding out my ring size is a breeze for Valerie, who seductively caresses my hands, pressing and sliding her thumb and forefinger down my fingertips. Valerie doesn't have to be super-hot to stir something inside me. And stir something inside Deb as she shoots a stink eye my way, warning me that I'm liking this too much. Maybe Valerie's touch isn't very seductive. More like clinical. But contact is contact.

I know it.

Deb knows it, too. In between stink eyes, she asks whether the store does custom engraving. I expect Deb to suggest "Together forever" or "With all my heart," but she wants to know the cost to etch "Put it back on." Can't you just feel the "love, honor, and obey" in her query? Or just the "for better or worse" coming out?

Valerie, on the other hand, just wants to do her job without some goofball thumping his foot on the floor like a trick horse being asked the square root of nine. Clomp. Clomp. Clomp.

"A perfect ten," Valerie exclaims.

"Why, thank you." I blush. "But the ring?"

Valerie ignores my charms.

"Ten's your ring size. Which is great because all of our display rings are size ten."

"Great." I sigh.

"Great." Deb smiles.

"Great." Valerie cha-chings.

I slip on a few rings. And, yes, they fit quite nicely. I politely smile when I finally get to contort my neck enough to see the prices that were magically hidden inside the display case, in between the felt ring holders, and under Valerie's thumb.

Did I really expect it to cost less than Deb's? Of course not. I know I shouldn't, but I must.

"So do you ever have a sale here? Maybe even a buy-one-get-one-free day?" I ask.

Valerie chuckles.

However, the poor bastard trying on rings with his fiancée a few feet away gives me a big belly laugh.

"No sales like that at Tiffany's," Valerie admits.

"Any irregulars?" I ask. "I know Deb's engraving desires, but I'm open. Fred. Joe. Bill. I've been called worse."

"Sorry, no irregulars."

"Except you and me," the other groom-to-be shouts out.

"You know it!" I shout back. "Yeow!"

Yeow? An old frat call of mine? Football cheer? Rock lyric? Nope. Deb just slammed her heel into my foot.

My head drops in shame. The other guy's drops as well. At least I can only guess his does, for I dare not look up just yet.

"We'll think it over," I politely mumble to Valerie. Head still down.

Deb politely pulls me aside. Fortunately, Tiffany's is prepared for this type of conversation. There are nooks and crannies throughout the store to allow discreet conversations to take place. I feel one of those discreet conversations coming on right now.

"What do you mean, 'we'll think it over'?" Deb says. Not so discreetly, I might add.

"Look, be happy you're taken care of. Let me worry about myself."

"Don't tell me to be happy. You need a ring. And don't think you're going to get away without getting, or wearing, one. This is one of our deals. Remember?"

"I remember. I wear a ring and you take my name. By the way, how is the DMV change application going?"

"Get the ring. Then you'll get your name."

"Trust me. I'll get a ring."

Deb gives me another look. Not the stop-flirting-with-Valerie-stink-eye look. A deeper, darker, more aggressive look. Pit bulls stop dead in their tracks from that look. Trees lose their leaves. In summer. From that look. Thankfully, she spares my other foot from getting a heel slam.

We return to a still-smiling, obviously-knowing Valerie to pick up Deb's ring. Blue box, white ribbon, Tiffany's bag and all.

I fumble with the bag while Deb's already at another counter picking out the tenth-anniversary diamond tennis bracelet I'll be buying her. That's the modern anniversary gift. If we were to go traditional, I'd have fifty extra years to afford that gift. But, I won't hold my breath on that one. She's also looking at the diamond earrings she'll be receiving after giving birth to our first child. The one I won't be able to afford after buying those earrings.

Damn you, Front of Tiffany's!

"How much for just the box?" I whisper to Valerie.

"Pardon?"

"Do you ever just sell the box?" Okay, I admit it's a long shot. But I really don't care where my ring comes from.

Valerie doesn't take my question in the lighthearted, "hey I'm just kidding" way. As long as she doesn't press the security buzzer below the countertop, I'll be fine.

"So, is there only one Dumpster for a store this size? Because that's where you might throw out any broken boxes, right?"

Now Valerie reaches for that buzzer.

And Deb, after hearing my last question, reaches for me. More like lunges. But contact is contact.

We leave the store. Deb with her pretty blue box. And me with my bruised purple arm. Deb's not sure how to react. Her ring is sorted, but she is worried my ring will fall into my bottomless in-box of wedding things to do.

"Sweetie, I promise I'll get a ring tonight," I profess in the car ride home. "Look how pretty that blue box is . . ."

"You'd better. They had nice ones."

"Which is great if I wear it all the time." Did I really say that? Maybe she didn't hear me.

"What did you just say?" She heard.

"I want it to be great since I'll wear it all the time."

No reaction. I'd better buy a ring tonight, especially since I want some credit for getting her wedding band so quickly and without much fuss. Visible fuss, that is. Inside I'm fuming about dropping a grand for something that looks like it wouldn't even keep a sink faucet from leaking.

✧

ONCE HOME, I race straight to the computer. "Go ahead, I'll eat in a minute," I shout out.

Think, Craig. Think.

Fifteen minutes later, I buy my ring. Bless the Internet. Where else can you search on "cheap platinum wedding band cheap cheap" and procure the ring of your dreams? Five-millimeter. Domed. Comfort fit. Size ten (thanks Valerie). If you don't know what all this means, that's okay. Neither do I. But in five to seven business days I'll find out. And the online store promises to ship it in a blue box. What color blue is anyone's guess.

I can't wait a week to get credit for this monumental to-do. I casually drop the e-receipt on Deb's lap. "Ahem," is all I say.

Sparks fly. Lips mash. Bodies join.

Guess it is really hump day after all.

ALREADY BOUGHT THE RING?

DON'T THINK YOU'RE done with Tiffany & Co. just yet. Or ever. Many wedding anniversaries demand (er, dictate; er, suggest) that the ideal gift for your mate comes in a little box and is sold by people behind big glass cases.

Year	Traditional	Modern
1	Paper	Clocks
2	Cotton	China
3	Leather	Glass
4	Linen	Appliances
5	Wood	Silverware
6	Iron	Wood
7	Wool	Desk sets
8	Bronze	Linens
9	Pottery	Leather
10	Aluminum	Diamond
11	Steel	Fashion jewelry
12	Silk	Pearls
13	Lace	Furs
14	Ivory	Gold jewelry
15	Crystal	Watches
20	China	Platinum
25	Silver	Silver
30	Pearl	Diamond
35	Jade	Jade
40	Ruby	Ruby
45	Sapphire	Sapphire
50	Gold	Gold
55	Emerald	Emerald
60	Diamond	Diamond

And don't forget jewelry for births, birthdays, and just about any time you're in the doghouse.

HERE'S THE RING.
NO TAKE-BACKS?
THAT'S WHAT SHE THINKS.

UNLIKE BIRTHDAY OR holiday gifts, courts usually view engagement rings as a conditional gift that only vests with the recipient when a marriage actually takes place. If the marriage fails to occur, the vesting also fails. In these instances, the person who gives the ring should expect it back, unless he broke the engagement without legal justification (e.g., he cheated with another woman).

To increase your rights to get The Rock back if things go rocky, avoid proposing on normally gift-giving days, including birthdays, Valentine's Day, and Christmas. And if you want to be doubly protected, work some "conditional gift" language in the proposal itself. Hey, no one ever said legalese makes for romance. For even more insurance, say all of this in front of others who can serve as witnesses for your defense. Or at your funeral.

Women have been known to accuse their mates of breach of contract if they didn't marry them. By now, most states have laws in place to prevent these suits. But there are still a few places that allow pain and suffering charges to be filed against a third party (e.g., his mistress) who caused the breakup. Did someone say "meow?"

WILL YOU TAKE MY HAND . . . AND HOLD IT WHILE I PUKE?

A man who wants a happy marriage should learn to keep his mouth shut and his checkbook open.
(Groucho Marx)

SINCE DEB'S TAKING a break from the working world to go back to school for her nursing degree (I'm still waiting for those "practice sponge baths" homework), I am the sole breadwinner for the Michaels duo. And, as the sole breadwinner, I make it a point to constantly appear busy while at my desk. I definitely look busy, but it's only because I'm giving our wedding Web site (craiganddeb.com) a much-needed upgrade. The Web site is the one wedding task that I have taken charge of and executed beyond all expectations. Anything for fifteen minutes of fame.

My work diversion is unfortunate for my company, but a bonanza for my cyberfans waiting for the next update. I couldn't imagine any of them getting sleep until knowing where our rehearsal dinner is going to be held. Okay, there are just six Web addicts: Deb, my mom, Deb's mom, Rick, and two strangers who signed our virtual guest book with "Call us when you get bored. In bed."

I add a few wedding weekend updates, some new pictures, and finally get around to posting the infamous proposal video.

THE PROPOSAL. ONE of my crowning achievements, even if the details are a bit hazy to both of us. (My advice on proposing should be self-evident: lay off the booze that night, both before and after the question. Or make sure your friends have a steady hand with the camcorder.) But isn't that how most great stories are made?

We were throwing a joint New Year's Eve and birthday party for me. Deb went all out with the food, drinks, and a huge cake. Her plan was to gather at our house and then head out to see English Beat perform (ah, to be products of the eighties . . .).

Little did Deb know her engagement ring arrived a few days before the party (Ring Tip Number 4.5: ship The Rock across state lines to avoid taxes). I cleverly hid it inside a decade-old box of computer cables. Deb would never poke around that mess. And it doesn't matter that I can't keep a secret because I was playing with a video camera Deb gave me as an early birthday gift. No time to spill the beans when you're trying to make it to Sundance next year.

My plan was that once my birthday cake came out, everyone would expect me to say a few words and then, BAM, I would propose. Genius. I even memorized a few romantic things to say just in case I went speechless. But I wasn't really worried. As soon as I looked into Deb's eyes, I knew it would all make sense.

At the party, everyone was drinking and having a good time, hosts included. Well, hosts especially. Drew had my camera, trying to catch all the action. Not that he or anyone else knew what I was planning. People were getting antsy, wanting to go to the concert. But Deb hadn't served the cake yet. Apparently, she was enjoying the party too much (read: liquored) to remember. And I was busy calming my nerves (read: liquored) to remind her. People started to leave. I started to panic.

"Hey. It's my birthday and I got something to say," I shouted out. Not what I practiced, but it would have to do.

I bent down (more like fell over) on one knee and pulled out the ring. Luckily, I had taken the ring out of the computer tub before raising my first glass that evening or else I might have tried to wrap a serial cable around Deb's finger.

"Deb, I love you and want you to be mine forever," came out of my mouth. Not the more standard "Will you marry me?" that should have been etched in my brain by now. I also managed to put the ring on her wrong hand (left hand good, right hand bad), even after secretly practicing that maneuver on myself at least a hundred times in the bathroom.

In a single swoop, Deb corrected the ring-hand problem, accepted my lame proposal, and kissed me. It's as if she secretly practiced making me look good for just this occasion. "I would be proud to be your wife," she professed. A bit stunned by the timing, but not the request.

Don't ask me what anyone else was really doing at that moment. I was too busy keeping my balance. And not just physically (even though gravity ultimately won). Emotionally, I was torn between releasing the tears because I was so happy and being a stoic man, casually moving on with life (tears won). Psychologically, I tried not to see myself twenty years from now, and I just tried to enjoy the moment for the moment's sake (time machine won; I'm going to turn really gray).

But, thanks to the miracle of videotape, I was able to enhance my memory of the events. Not sure the look on everyone's face could be called an enhancement, but they did cheer for us after a good ten seconds of shock and awe.

After toasts and hugs, we did leave to see the band. Or that was what the others told me. I blacked out shortly after the proposal. The next thing I vaguely remember was rushing the stage during "Tenderness." I definitely remember the bouncers could have been more tender themselves as they removed me from the stage.

I woke up New Year's Day with an amazing hangover and a black eye (thanks, kind bouncers). As I cracked open my good eye, I saw Deb staring at me, ring on the correct hand. Smile across her face. Okay, she was staring at the ring and I just happened to be in the background, but I felt her love. Then I threw up. Then she threw up. Then I threw up again.

✧

OUR WEDDING SITE also has a countdown timer. Just under two million seconds to go. "No need to worry until we're down to around two hundred and fifty thousand. That's when we'll be in Vegas," I offer while telling Deb my Web work is done for the day.

She then tells me we're talking finances tonight.

Now it's time to worry.

✧

NO ONE WILL EVER quote me in the *Wall Street Journal*. And Deb's not a Warren Buffet in drag. But, any finance talk we have will be fine. I totally believe that we should share our misfortunes. And it's a good thing our families are so squarely middle-class, lest we have to worry about any pesky inheritances to misinvest.

Our biggest laugh, and cry, comes while reviewing Deb's stock portfolio. Or should I say stock. She was an early employee at a company that went from pennies to hundreds of dollars a share. And then back to pennies. And then we sold. Ironically, the stock hit its high right about the time we met. I would have told her to sell if I'd known, I tell myself in retrospect. Who knew she was smart, pretty, and filthy rich? But I'll gladly settle for two out of three.

We settle on keeping separate checking accounts for now, but agree to open a joint account for all of our wedding loot. (Please let there be wedding loot.) Over time, our individuality (read: separate ATM PINs) will cease to be and all monies would eventually merge into one nest egg. But by then, the Dow will be over twenty thousand. Mark my financial-whiz-kid words.

SAVE YOURSELF TWO HUNDRED DOLLARS AN HOUR. SOME LEGAL INFO.

WHILE YOU MAY think marriage is all about romance, passion, and cake, there are some governmental fine points that need to be accounted for. For the majority of states, marriage begins once the ceremony ends. However, a few will let you slip in an annulment if things haven't been consummated yet.

Ceremonial marriages are the most common way to get hitched. In a ceremonial marriage, you present the marriage license to an authorized state official (e.g., judge, court clerk, or clergy member). The official will then perform the ceremony and issue a marriage certificate. A promise to marry is all that's required in the ceremony. After that, you're free to include or exclude anything you want.

Common-law marriages are only recognized by a few states. It's not enough for you to live with someone for an extended period of time in order to be considered in a common-law marriage. You and your mate have to present yourselves as husband and wife to all that cross your path. Even so, odds are your state doesn't allow common-law marriages due to the potential for misunderstandings and fraud, so get with the program and print a program (wedding program, that is).

Other types of marriages that may be legal include the proxy marriage (someone stands in for a partner that is unable to be physically present due to prison or military duty), confidential marriages (no witnesses are required), and marriages of convenience (the underlying reason for the relationship isn't love).

Marriages that aren't allowed are ones that result from fraud, occur between close relatives, or include underage individuals.

While it is expected for a married couple to live together, it is not legally required. But don't think that's a free pass for extracurricular activities. Adultery is illegal in many states.

Not getting enough? Or any? There's hope. Or help. If your spouse snubs all sexual attempts (without good cause), you can use "constructive abandonment" as grounds for divorce. Hopefully, it'll never get this far. May I suggest doing something other than raising your eyebrows to get her in the mood?

Can pillow talk stay just between you and your mate? You bet. In most states, either spouse can refuse to testify against each other or discuss their private conversations. Unless she's really mad at you. Or it's really embarrassing. Then you're probably out of luck.

■

THE WEDDING PARTY: STRENGTH IN NUMBERS

TODAY IT MIGHT be about giving your buddies easier access to cute bridesmaids. But in ancient times, groomsmen were there to guarantee a wedding took place. Back in the days when a groom would have to capture his bride, he would call on his friends to help keep the peace with the bride's family.

To confuse any evil spirits intending to harm the bride and groom, the wedding party dressed like the happy couple. How many identically-dressed people did it take to bamboozle the evil spirits in the old days? Ten. An open bar didn't hurt, either.

Traditionally, your brother should serve as best man. If you have more than one brother, choose the one that beat you up least. If they all beat the crap out of you, pick the oldest. If you don't have any brothers and your sisters didn't leave you emotionally crippled without buddies, select your best friend to be best man. Just make sure he's a stand-up (and not drink until he throws up) kind of guy.

As far as groomsmen go, you should first ask your remaining brothers as well as your fiancée's brothers. Then, your friends. Finally, other relatives. While it's nice to ask people whose wedding you were in, don't be forced into a large wedding party just to pay back others. In lieu of being a groomsman, you can ask someone to perform a reading during the ceremony or hand out programs.

The (Occasionally) Lost Weekend

My wife doesn't care what I do when I'm away,
as long as I don't have a good time.
(Lee Trevino)

I SPRING OUT of bed with a bounce not felt for ages. Did I finally get a restful night's sleep? Did Deb stay up and finish all of my to-do's? Better yet, did time fast-forward to after the wedding and all turned out amazingly well? Nope. But I shall feel no worries today. I am immune to planning despair. My bachelor party weekend begins tonight!

Ah, the Bachelor Party (an event that, to many, ranks up there with Labor Day, Christmas, Ramadan, Kwanzaa, Rosh Hashanah, the advent of the Tooth Fairy, and New Year's Eve as national holidays, needed to be recognized by all). Since the dawn of time, men and women have joined together in marriage to preserve and ensure the continuity of the human race. And right before such for-ever-and-ever, ever-after togetherness would occur, men have banded as one to bid farewell to the Bachelor's Good Life. Whether it entailed chest-beating and lounging about in caves, drinking Caveman Lite and leering at carvings of naked women frolicking (yes, historians have proved that the lesbian mystique haunted Cro-Magnon man) or chest-beating and lounging about in the *Real World* suite at The Palms, drinking Bud Lite and leering at three-dimensional naked women frolicking, the basic premise has remained the same: testosterone, alcohol, money, women, embarrassment, and tall tales to those who didn't attend. Man might have evolved from single cells to upright thinkers, but bachelor parties? Why fix what's not broken?

While I could only imagine what Fred Flintstone's party was like, I wasn't going to go into this weekend as a red-blooded, unwedded American male without having done my research. And research I did. Relying on the best-quality resources, those of superb intellect and far reach, the very annals of maledom: *Bachelor Party* with Tom Hanks, *Very Bad Things* with Christian Slater, every issue of *FHM,* my well-hidden porn collection, and half the Internet for some basic rules of a bachelor party:

- Everything is paid for by your buddies (even the cheapest of skates)
- You magically possess six-pack abs, a full head of hair, and pearly white teeth
- You wear a toga for at least half the night ("long live" constantly precedes your name)
- No fewer than ten women throw themselves on you (literally and figuratively)
- No fewer than ten kegs are consumed
- You reek of moisturizer and glow from glitter (stripper glitter, not the arts-and-crafts kind)
- No fewer than three farm animals are present (but not harmed)
- There's no wait at any bar (you are a very, very, so very VIP)
- Guiltless sex abounds (not going to touch that one . . .)

Are my expectations a bit excessive? Am I playing into the stereotypical male fantasy? Will Deb's bachelorette party follow similar tenets? Should I be more scared of this coming true for Deb than for it coming true for me?

Of course, these party rules, unlike wedding vows, are meant to be broken. Especially considering the source of my party planning. I love my friends, but "successful social planner" is definitely not on their resumes. Even if I were to discount my expectations from "ultimate" to "average" (read: scantily-clad ladies prancing around a gigantic suite at Bellagio), I might still be disappointed.

Being the semi-able-bodied male that I actually am, I really only asked for only one thing at the bachelor party: a roast. An old-fashioned, cigar-smoking, anything-goes, drinking-all-around, everyone-standing-up-and-knocking-me-down roast. Deb nixed the idea for a couple's roast at our rehearsal dinner. I was "doing enough to poke fun at the wedding" as it was. It's probably better for the ribbing to take place in the privacy of men. As is customary in a roast, the roastee gets a turn to roast the roasters. I haven't been reading the biographies of Henny Youngman, Alan King, and Don Rickles for nothing. My suitcase is packed with index cards full of return jabs.

But, who am I kidding? They'll have nothing ready for me. I'll have to slip them a few just to be sure:

> Craig's so hairy, he wears an all-over shower cap.
> Craig's a modest person, with much to be modest about.
> Craig's as organized as a soup sandwich.
> Craig and I have been through so much together. And most of it was his fault.
> Craig found his true love. Too bad he can't marry himself.

✧

I LEAVE IN an hour. I'm still knee-deep in clothes debating what to wear that doesn't scream "soon to be married." Unfortunately, most of my clothes are some flavor of plaid. Apparently, I'm already married.

Deb sneaks up from behind. "What'cha doing?" she asks.

"Packing."

"What'cha want to be doing?"

"Packing."

"Anything else you what'cha want to be doing?"

"What's with the what'chas?"

Frustrated, Deb grabs me below the belt. Unexpected? Yes. Welcomed? Oh yeah. Worried that I'll be time-constrained as a result of our passionate lovemaking? Nah.

We're done, and I still have a good fifty-five minutes left to pack.

"Was that what'cha wanted?" I cheerfully ask.

"More or less."

What bride-to-be in her right mind would send her groom-to-be off to a mysterious land of naked ladies without one for the road? Every man should take advantage of this phenomenon. This makes twice for the week, a post-engagement, pre-wedding, all-time high. But I have no time to think about that now. I have lots more on my mind. Finding the least-offending plaid shirt is a real brainteaser.

✧

OUR DESTINATION IS twofold: Lake Tahoe, a great cover for the bachelor party, and Reno, where most of the debaucheries will take place. Reno works for three key reasons: it's sinful, it's drivable, and it's not Vegas. I feel it's important to keep the wedding and bachelor party venues separate.

"Nothing ruins a wedding faster than one of the servers at our Vegas reception recognizing you as the jerk who couldn't keep his pants on at the blackjack table," I tell Rick on the way to the cabin.

We arrive at around midnight. Tonight is for gambling. Gambling to increase our weekend slush fund. Well, I am gambling to increase my Deb gift fund. I have a feeling that I'll be paying off this trip well beyond the twenty-dollar lap dances on tap for tomorrow. Roast aside, and now that I'm here, I figure it's my duty to capture as much of the Ultimate Bachelor Party as possible. I hope I packed my toga. And gold-leaf headpiece.

"Guys. Please don't mention to anyone it's my wedding." I am pathetic as we head toward the CalNeva casino.

"What about the big dildo we got for your forehead?" Rick questions.

Apparently, Rick's crashed too many bachelorette parties where the bride-to-be wears a plastic penis hat and dances with a life-size, wish-it-was-real, inflatable Mr. Perfect (always ready to listen, won't want sex until she does, will wear whatever she suggests). "Please. Mum's the word?" How much of my desperation is now appearing?

"We'll see, Mister Bachelor."

Fate is clearly out of my hands.

✧

AFTER TWO HOURS of breaking even at craps, we head to a black-jack table and mosey up to some cuties drinking Long Island iced teas. *Cuties* is a relative term. We're drunk, and, relatively speaking, they're drunker. Nevertheless, we mingle. After five minutes, Sydney, the woman next to me, starts to leave.

"No more moo-ney," Sydney slurs. "Unless you back me up."

"Is that what the kids are calling it these days?"

"What?"

Am I am too old or just too dull? Thank God for Deb.

"Soooo, should I stay?" Sydney asks.

"Of course." We are only at the five-dollar table. I slide a twenty across the green felt. Who says chivalry is dead?

Within minutes, I get Sydney's whole life story. Her family owns half of winery-rich Sonoma County. She's spending the summer getting away from all those luxuries and pressures. My heart bleeds for her. She's twenty-two. My heart bleeds for me. What would life be like with a twenty-two-year-old wine heiress as my wife? Nonstop naked grape-stomping? Happy hop-skips-and-jumps though our vineyards? Blowout bashes at our hilltop mansion (on land that's value increases an order of magnitude every three years)? I could see it. I could be it. I could really fall for Deb. Deb?

Deb. Nothing crashes a bachelor party moment faster than mixing your real wife-to-be with your make-believe-wife-not-to-be.

A few hands later, the heiress reveals even more. "You know, I haven't had good sex in a year," Sydney whispers.

"I don't think tonight will change that."

Finally it hits her. "Oh, you must have a girlfriend."

Unconsciously, I smile.

"Wait. You're getting married, aren't you?" she adds. Psychic? Psycho?

Consciously, I frown.

"Oh my god. This is your bachelor party." To everyone, Sydney announces, "It's his bachelor party."

Not that it matters now, but I know a one-night stand would be out of the question. Even if I wanted to seek vengeance for all my previously blown one-nighters. (Eight to be exact, but who's counting?)

I do, however, continue to flirt with Sydney. Why not? Sydney's too drunk to remember what she just learned about me. And it beats talking to Rick, who is on fire at the table. But it's tough to flirt when you're the only one talking. Sydney's focus is on the essentials: sitting, breathing, and occasionally blinking.

I know the hand I've been dealt. I leave with a good-luck-getting-married kiss. Plus one-hundredth of an acre of prime Sonoma property in exchange for the sixty dollars I ultimately lent Syndey. It's an official document. What court would reject a deed written on a cocktail napkin and witnessed by Abe, our friendly pit boss?

Abe thinks I should have gone for the one-night stand. "House rules," Abe cites.

Obviously Abe doesn't live at my house.

Dateline 5:30 AM
Day 2 of Lost Weekend. Inside a Lake Tahoe cabin.

ONE WOULD THINK that after experiencing such a losing evening at the blackjack table on my first night of the bachelor party, God would at least reward me with a good night's sleep. She didn't. All night I tossed and turned, pondering life's great issues of the day. What did I really lose last night? Money? Not that much. Manhood? Again, not that much, but that could have been my last fling. Does Deb have these thoughts, too? Does she think I would jeopardize what we have built together for anyone? Anyone besides our three already-agreed-upon sleepover celebrities (me: Sarah Jessica Parker, Jennifer Garner, and Elizabeth Hurley; her: Russell Crow, Jimmy Fallon, and Jude Law). Does she think I can succumb to the call of a mildly attractive (but very rich, remember) siren? Do I give her reason to worry?

I finally reach an acceptable hour to phone Deb.

"Why are you calling?" she asks.

"I love you," I say.

"What did you do wrong? Who have you slept with?" The pace of her voice quickens. "Just tell me. We can work it out."

"Whoa. I was just thinking about you and us. You know, how I can't wait to get married."

"Liar. I hope you are alone. It'd be really crummy if you were saying that with some slut passed out next to you."

"No slut. Just Drew."

"You know, we shouldn't be talking," Deb says. "It's your last time to go wild. See tits. Drink."

Click.

Have I mentioned how much I love Deb?

I STRUGGLE TO get out of bed for call number two. Already out of cash, I don't think my three-hundred-dollar ATM limit will sustain me this evening. Unfortunately, Linda, my bank's customer support rep, can't seem to grasp my sudden need for greenbacks.

"Mr. Michaels. You know your ATM card can be used as a charge or debit card almost anywhere."

"But I just need more cash."

"The closest bank open on a Saturday is in Sacramento."

"That's not really close."

"Again, sir, your merchants would be happy to take your card. Or you could write a check."

"I'd prefer not to."

"I am sorry, but I just don't understand."

And at this moment, Drew wakes up and lets out a rant to no one in particular, but audible throughout the Sierra Nevada mountains. "I can't believe I'm down four hundred bucks and I haven't seen one naked girl!" Thousands of birds, fish, and animals just got spooked, thinking they're about to be someone's breakfast.

Silence ensues. Drew farts. More silence.

Linda speaks. "Now, Mr. Michaels, you can upgrade your checking account to Premier Gold status which would give you a higher daily allowance for any, um, immediate spending requirements."

Way to go, Linda.

FOR A SECOND-ORDER alibi (you can never be too careful at your bachelor party), however weak it may be, to all our womenfolk back home, we kayak around Lake Tahoe. And go for a swim. It's more like a jump, as the water here never rises above fifty degrees. My girly shrieks ruin this wonderful man's-man moment we were about to have.

As I adjust to the lake's temperature, my manhood shrinks to near oblivion and my pre-wedding worry rises to rampant levels. Or, could the wedding worries be the true cause of my shrinkage? What will married life be like? Will I have the same freedoms as I enjoy now? Who am I kidding? I've been in relationships 99 percent of my adult life. Freedom is a state of mind. Deb has always encouraged me to maintain my own individuality. I am not sure if I've ever fully taken her up on that or have been using our relationship as a crutch.

Who knows what the future will hold? Starting a family has a lot more obligations than a having a permanent Saturday night date. But isn't that what I really want? Nay, really need? Scenes of my future flash before me:

- Changing diapers. The room smells like a sulfur mine. I'm smiling.
- With our extended family under a Christmas tree lighted by menorahs. I don't get the AG-DVX100B high-definition camcorder I've hinted at for the last six months. I'm smiling.

- Giving our daughter (yes, Deb got her wish) her first driving lesson. We have just suffered a few thousand dollars of body damage. I'm smiling.
- Taking pictures of our daughter as she leaves for her first prom with a guy who suspiciously reminds me of myself. And even though I thoroughly checked her date for flasks, I'm not smiling. Not smiling at all.
- Underneath a "Happy 50th Anniversary" banner. We're all wrinkled and hard of hearing. I'm smiling.

None of the other guys notice that I've been staring into space for the past five minutes, smiling like an idiot. They couldn't care less. Bastards.

WE BARBEQUE STEAKS and feast like kings. And now I can't wait to be served up for dessert. But it seems that dessert is lame-duck pudding.

"Roast me!" I proclaim.

"You suck!" Rick yells.

"You're fat!" Patrick shouts.

"Take a shower!" Jake quips.

"Don't you watch Comedy Central? Or even the Three Stooges? You could at least throw a pie at me. You're pathetic," I lament. "I haven't asked any of you for anything. And this is what I get? Deb's crew is available seven days a week. They talk. They cry. They plan. They share. What about me? I have needs, too. Do you guys even care?"

For the second time today, I sit in silence for what seems like an eternity. Then a break.

"Reno," Patrick offers.

"Reno," Rick seconds.

"Reno. Reno. Reno," everyone proclaims.

Sigh. "Reno, baby, Reno," I quietly accept. And understand. Men aren't programmed the same way as women. We're binary with decisions. Logical with reasoning. Uncomfortable with emotions. These guys are giving me as much as they can. And that's fine by me. After all, even an emotional wreck like me shouldn't stay too worked up over this.

Before leaving San Francisco, Deb made me promise one thing: no strippers were allowed to make house calls. We could go to as many places as we could handle, but by no means were we allowed to host our own private party. That's reasonable. I saw no need to tell my friends as that type of coordination was way beyond their means. Why sound henpecked for no reason? Except that I am now being informed of our first destination: a suite at the Flamingo. The girls will be arriving shortly. Good, but bad. Thrilling, but chilling. Am I at the threshold of the Ultimate Bachelor Party? Am I about to bear witness to a multiple-girl fest? And are they going to serve up a big Craig sandwich? Will I simultaneously, miraculously also win every round of 21, craps, and roulette in the place? Will every slot machine spill its gold to the tune of "Craig! Craig! Craig, you lucky dog!"

Deb is so going to kick my ass.

✧

AT THE SUITE, we drink Buds and watch ESPN. Manly things to do. Our high-fives and "boo-yeas" get interrupted by a knock at the door. Two women. Nice. Jake and Rick spring up to negotiate. Note to self: Jake and Rick are the ringleaders. Blame them. Always blame someone.

Since our suite isn't really that big, the required "paperwork" needs to be filled out in the bathroom. Classy. Where did these women come from? Did the gentlemen, my esteemed friends, meet them before? Are they aspiring dental students? I shouldn't know. Any additional details would just make it harder to maintain the already big-ass lie I'm going to have to tell Deb. And swear the guys to, too.

After a few calls from the bathroom to the Stripper Home Office to verify the credit card is valid, they emerge. Summer, a beautiful redhead, and Lexi, a sultry brunette. Perfect stripper names. Perfect stripper bodies. Perfect stripper boots with six-inch stripper heels. A perfect start to a perfect night.

I am tossed in the middle of the room. Very classy.

What proceeds can only be described as simultaneously one of the most sexy and sexless situations of my life. Yes, there are two women gyrating all around me, but there are also fourteen eyes staring at me. Granted, those eyes are probably focused elsewhere, but I feel a bit uncomfortable in the center of it all. Not "run home and tell my fiancée" uncomfortable, so I shrug it off and groove to the music playing from the hotel clock radio. So very, very classy.

Things progress, but are still a bit off. I cannot put my finger on it. And I dare not put my finger on Summer, lest some angry men come find me. I scan the room. The guys are idly sitting around. Neither Summer nor Lexi is really working the room. And they aren't really working me, either. They're just drifting around.

The radio starts to play the Bee Gees. Couldn't Drew find a better station? One with lyrics like "shake that ass," "be my bitch," or "guys with glasses are hot"? This is not worth the beating I am going to get at home.

Finally, Summer leans in to me. I sit back and wait for the dirty talk to begin. "Your friends really don't like you, do they?"

What is she talking about? Does she know about the roast—or lack thereof?

"What's wrong with them?" Summer's getting upset. And the last thing I want to see is an upset stripper. Even if she sucks at her job.

Now everyone's antsy—especially Summer. I'd like to say I figured the situation out on my own, but Lexi is kind enough to clue me in on the missing details. Well, one missing detail.

"You know, we're hookers."

"One more time," I say.

"Hookers. Your friends are supposed to leave us alone. So we can have a good time."

"Sorry, just one more time." Yes, this is new to me. I swear this is new to me. So, I'm off to a rocky start, but I'm still on the playing field of the Ultimate Bachelor Party. Why didn't I memorize the playbook more? Am I supposed to run a pick and roll? Double-play? Hail Mary (wait, it's Hail Summer and Lexi)?

"Too late. Your hour is up. Your loss," Summer chimes in.

Game over. Summer and Lexi have left the building. I am shut down, out, and upped.

The seven of us, with more IQ power than most rural towns, an intimate knowledge of working a Reverse Polish Notation calculator (big boy math), fifteen advanced degrees, and arguably a million dollars in combined annual salary, could not figure out that these ladies were hookers for an hour. Talk about being book smart with no street sense.

After being so abruptly disqualified from an Ultimate Bachelor Party moment, I have to wonder: was this really my loss? Years from now, will I look back, slumped in my La-Z-Boy, remote control on my belly, wondering what I missed? Did I miss my calling? The one chance at the big leagues?

No, this is my gain. I'm not going to sleep with a hooker just before my wedding. Now, two hookers? Hmm. Still no. Three? Well, let's just say I'm glad there weren't three. Every mortal man has his price.

Being a good sport, I laugh it off, grateful everyone got to share in the embarrassment. And even more grateful that I had a room full of witnesses to my gentlemanly behavior to back me up when word gets out.

On to the preapproved-by-Deb part of my bachelor party: strip joints.

Dateline 10:01 AM
Day 3 of Lost Weekend. On a Trail Along Lake Tahoe.

NOT MY BEST morning, but, fortunately, a self-diagnosis reveals the following:

- No permanent tattoos, unless you count five hand stamps from Reno's best strip joints
- No deliberate body piercing, but a few paper cuts from my five ATM receipts
- No wedding rings, but I vaguely remember tossing out a few proposals

- All of my teeth, although some feel ready to drop out of the desert my mouth has become
- A deep pain in my chest, but just a few sore ribs thanks to a fuzzy recollection of some Amazon strippers from hell

I survived. And as such, I shall resist my urge to call Deb. She is probably busy getting ready for her bridal shower today anyway. Her sister is hosting a full, action-packed day of gabbing, ring-gawking, and gift-opening. No need to add groom-bashing to the list. Okay, extra groom-bashing. I'm sure that I already made it on the agenda.

While the other guys remain comatose, I go for a run along the lake. Not too far. Just enough to sweat some alcohol and collect my thoughts.

Well, there's only enough energy for one thought: my body isn't made for these nights anymore. It clearly is time for me to settle down with the girl of my dreams. I know her recent nagging is only temporary and, once the wedding's over, the easygoing, fun-loving woman who everyone wants to be around will emerge from the ceremonial rice and flowers. But how could I make this life transition happen in the blink of an eye?

A quickie Bar Mitzvah? Dropping out of Hebrew School on my second day makes this a bit tough to pull off at this moment. A heartfelt church confession? While there are probably many priests eager to hear my Reno sins, I'm still not sure how those booths really work (do I need exact change?). A Yom Kippur fasting? Still got a few months before this kicks in. A pretend-it-was-just-Yom-Kippur-and-have-a-fast-breaking feast? I could bathe myself in a purifying breakfast of eggs over easy, waffles, hash, biscuits, pigs in a blanket (the full-size kind), and gravy, but something tells me I would pay for that longer than is called for.

There must be a simpler out-with-the-old-in-with-the-new gesture I can perform. And like sirens calling for Ulysses, the clear blue ice-cold water of Tahoe calls for me. I can't resist. I must not resist. There's not even time to pull my Nikes off.

"Yow!"

I am not a religious person by any means, but this feels baptismal. I am in the middle of a supersized cleansing process. My body is being freed of all my evil bachelor spirits and deeds. Not just from the previous night, but the last thirty years of previous nights. All that boozing, scamming, going home with a stranger, explaining who I am when they sober up, and trying to spy a phone number off a bill on the kitchen table before getting tossed out . . . no more.

This feels good. Righteous. Just. I am ready to get married. Ready to be a good husband. Ready to do some last-minute wedding details. Yow is right. I need to get cheated by hookers more often.

Dateline 10:08 AM
Day 3 of Lost Weekend, Back in the Cabin.

I'M A BIT soggy, but wiser. I see my friends with a new perspective—clutching onto hopeless fantasies of single life. Except for Drew. He's clutching onto the toilet.

Poor fools. They don't know the true meaning of love and commitment. I am complete. I am blessed. I am ready.

✧

AFTER DROPPING EVERYONE off, I fill up the car before heading home. The husband in me does this to be responsible, in case Deb wants to drive somewhere. The bachelor in me does it so I can douse myself with gasoline, to cover my tracks. Gas neutralizes the smell of cheap vanilla moisturizer and dampens the shine of any stripper glitter still clinging to my body.

My memories are dim. Thank goodness there were no cameras focused on me. At least none that I'm going to get a tape of. I pray none I'm (or worse, Deb's) going to get a tape of. But there were sparkly times, I think. I may not have been the direct target for all that glitter, but I was definitely in the brass pole "splash zone" at least a few times last night.

This glitter is tough stuff. Industrial adhesives aren't this binding. Even after my dip in the freezing lake, I look like a big-ass disco ball.

Alas, I accidentally swallowed some of Shell's finest eight-seven octane for naught. Deb's not home from her bridal shower yet. I scrub off in the tub, receiving my second baptism of the day. Not bad for the Jew without a Bar Mitzvah.

✧

DEB COMES HOME excited to see me. And I am happy to receive a hug from someone who truly means it. Not much is spoken about the weekend or the wedding. It is good to just relax on the couch and not be surrounded by mirrors, blinded from neon, or blasted with Aerosmith.

Another night of great sex. That's three this week if you count Sunday as ending the previous week. Which beats the hell out of the (physical, emotional, sexual, psychological, and financial) beating I took at the bachelor party. Guess I'm glad I didn't pack a toga. Or gold-leaf headpiece.

THE ONE PARTY THAT REALLY MATTERS: THE BACHELOR PARTY

THE AVERAGE BACHELOR party costs over one thousand dollars and includes ten men.

Thirsty? Not a problem. The average amount of beer consumed at a bachelor party is four cases.

Horny? Keep your fingers crossed. There is a one-in-three chance of seeing a stripper at the average bachelor party.

Jealous? You shouldn't be. Almost four out of five men claim they wouldn't mind if there was a male stripper at their fiancée's bachelorette party.

Source: "A Nice Ring to It," *Men's Health,* June 2002

Basic bachelor party rules
- Do have an alibi set up. Or at least a promise from everyone that mum's the word.
- Do buddy up (but don't worry if you lose him, especially when you're with your new buddy Amber).
- Do pay attention to the groom.
- Do embarrass the groom (get him tossed on stage, pointed at, and pushed into unsuspecting women).
- Do tell strip joints you're coming in advance (you might get a free limo, cover waived, or other "specials").
- Do know the difference between the Yellow Pages ad for a stripper and a prostitute. No moral judgment here . . . just making sure you read the fine print.
- Do have enough group money for bail.
- Do prepare for plenty of shots.
- Do roast groom. No need to have him full of self-confidence.
- Do spring for a proper hotel (even if you have to four-up in each room).

- ❥ Do fill the night with as many gag gifts as you can.
- ❥ Don't have party the night before the wedding. Do it one to three months before the big day.
- ❥ Don't drink and drive. Book a limo, flag down cabs, or designate a driver.
- ❥ Don't take pictures.
- ❥ Don't call fiancée during the party.
- ❥ Don't drop the groom off at his fiancée's afterwards.
- ❥ Don't bring up fiancée's name, even in a disrespectful way.

■

TRADITIONS TO START A MARRIAGE OFF RIGHT, BESIDES NOT SLEEPING WITH HOOKERS AT YOUR BACHELOR PARTY.

THE GROOM IS expected to carry his bride over the threshold into their new home. In Roman times, it was considered bad luck if the bride stumbled on her first entrance. Unfortunately, the Romans never said what to do when the groom is a klutz.

The best man used to tie tin cans to the back of the newlyweds' transportation to frighten away evil spirits. Now it's about less about spooking spirits and more about whooping and hollering to all within earshot.

In Jewish ceremonies, after the bride and groom drink a glass of wine, the groom wraps the glass in a napkin and smashes it with his foot. This act symbolizes the fall of the Temple of Jerusalem, a reminder that great joy can be suddenly shattered. Also, breaking glass cannot be undone, symbolizing the permanence of marriage.

It's good luck to marry on the groom's birthday, but never on the bride's. The best days to wed include Wednesday (guaranteed success), Thursday (great wealth), and Sunday (lasting love).

FEELING A BIT BACKED UP?

WAYS TO MAKE your fiancée re-enamored with you. Or at least keep the peace.

- Hold door open.
- Offer an unsolicited compliment.
- Let her sleep in late and make her breakfast in bed.
- Please her first . . . and last.
- Give her questions serious thought (then it's okay to say "whatever you think is best").
- Let her pick the movie, TV show, restaurant, or sex toy for the evening.
- Sneak up from behind and give her a neck rub.
- Yell at a wedding vendor on her behalf.
- Try on a bridesmaid dress if she asks (your manhood can take it).
- Play her favorite board game over candlelight and wine.
- Don't read, watch TV, or do work while eating dinner.
- Take her to the place you shared your first date.
- Surprise her at work and take her on a lunch date.
- Stay at a posh hotel one night.
- Suggest dinner at her parents' to discuss the wedding.

2

I CAN'T REST ON MY LAURELS. BECAUSE I DON'T HAVE ANY LAURELS.

Three weeks to go

New to-do's

Pour your heart out

Time to write your vows, speeches, and toasts. Or at least
copy and paste some sappy words from the Web. If you are
writing your own vows, try to include words like *love, cherish,
sacrifice, promise, infinite,* and *respect.* Avoid *pain, suffering,
one-way,* and *maybe.* And don't expect to just wing the
speeches and toasts, even if you are a funny drunk. You are
not a funny drunk.

80

Verify honeymoon reservations

Now's not the time to assume all is well with the honeymoon.
Expect the worst. Call the airlines, hotels, tour companies,
bars, and boogie board rental shacks. Make sure they know
you are coming.

You might want to order flowers, fresh fruit, and champagne
to be in your hotel room before you arrive. Or at least save
your bag of airplane peanuts. Okay, just steal hers.

Arrange with best man for ride from reception to airport

No, this isn't about a getaway car. Your best man should help
with ride arrangements from the reception to the airport (or
hotel if you are leaving the next day).

It's okay to rely on your best man for help with other things as
well. That's his job. Along with marrying your fiancée if you fail
to show up at the wedding.

to-do's

OLD TO-DO'S LEFT TO DO

How late am I?

Help choose bridal registry	8 months
Complete honeymoon plans	5 months
Attend dance lessons	2 months
Shop for honeymoon clothes	2 months
Check marriage license requirements	2 months
Help fiancée with Couple's Shower thank-you notes	2 months
Pick up wedding rings	2 months
Wine and dine her	1 week

day

HOW MUCH IS THAT CROCKERY IN THE WINDOW?

The trouble with some women is that they get all excited about nothing—and then marry him.
(Cher)

"FORGET HOW PRETTY the lake was, what about the hookers? Did you or didn't you?" Nico demands to know everything about the bachelor party.

"A gentleman never tells."

"You did!"

"I didn't! I swear I didn't. You better not tell Deb I did." I'm a gentleman no more. More like a scared little boy. "But I am a Sonoma landowner."

Our testosterone-charged conversation grinds to a halt as Deb's cell phone appears again on caller ID.

"I'm feeling domestic today, honey," Deb says.

Please mean housecleaning. "And that would entail . . ."

"Breaking out the slow cooker."

Ah, the slow cooker. One of our lovely shower gifts.

"That's, um, great."

"Craig. Every couple needs a slow cooker."

"But we already got a fast eater."

"Don't worry, I'll teach you how to use it."

"Any other domestic urges?" Please say cleaning.

"Well, we will be touching up the registry."

✧

WEDDING REGISTRIES ARE one of the best scams brides have pulled over the years. Their most recent advancement in roping their mates is the bar-code gun. Go to any department store and you'll see dozens of couples walking around with one of those guns. Now, look more closely. The girl is busy pointing out all the things she wants, and the guy happily aims and pulls the trigger, unaware that he isn't bustin' a cap in a wineglass, but permanently adding it (or twelve of them) to their cupboards. These items—goblets, flutes, snifters, gravy boats . . . you name it—along with 95 percent of the registry, will then forever be shipped, stored, unpacked, brought out, and cleaned when whoever gave you that gift pays a visit. But what other wedding activity resembles a video game? I can only imagine what's lurking inside the advanced technology labs at *Modern Bride*.

Deb and I came to a mutual agreement with regard to our registry. She decided, and I agreed:

China and glasses from Macy's. Relatively affordable one-hundred-dollar place settings for twelve. White with just a little platinum trim that hopefully won't go out of style before our reception date.

Household goodies from Crate and Barrel. Variety of shapes and prices, including a salad spinner, coffeemaker, and fondue set.

Two items of my choosing from Home Depot. After a happy hour roaming the orange aisles of Home Depot sans Deb, I decided on a Dremel (a multipurpose cut, slice, screw power thing) and a new Weber kettle grill (charcoal, never gas). I really don't need either. It's more like needing redemption from the other gifts we are about to receive.

I did have a brilliant registry idea that I imagine goes through the mind of every couple, who, like us (or like Deb), dismisses it out of poor taste. The idea is to put really expensive stuff on the registry and mark them as already bought. Out of guilt, our guests would have to upgrade whatever gifts they were going to buy. Sheer genius.

✧

NO SHOOT-'EM-UPS with a bar-code gun tonight, just clicking. We're logged on to crateandbarrel.com to add a few more registry items while discussing the merits of the choices.

"We can't have just one expensive pot, we need eight. How will it look to our dinner guests?"

"I understand completely."

Deb questions my sincerity. Actually, I am sincere. More like not worried. Because my ace in the hole is Patrick. I make a quick call to check up on Registry Plan B: The Groom Strikes Back. I knew I wasn't going to win any registry battle head-on. So Patrick and I picked one big-ticket item that's most important to me. Then Patrick planted this seed with my buddies, with a great deal of fertilizer in the form of less-than-subtle e-mail reminders. Never from me, of course. Plausible denial is key.

"It's been taken care of," Patrick says.

"Really?" I coyly ask.

"Relax. In a few weeks you'll be sitting in front of one big-ass big-screen TV, courtesy of your wedding."

"Deb can throw all the fancy parties she wants, with quality pots and platinum-trimmed china, but I'll be enjoying *Alias* in surround-o-vision every day."

"Just don't forget about reserving me a spot on your couch."

"I think there'll be plenty of room for you when Deb leaves me over this."

But Deb doesn't know yet, so I'm temporarily safe. She's all mine. And I crawl into bed and hug Deb tight, thanking her for saving me. That admission should be worth a few registry points at Home Depot. Shouldn't it?

OUR FOURTH TEA SET?
JUST WHAT WE ALWAYS WANTED.

THE REGISTRY IS meant to help the bride and groom get settled in her new home. Originally, the bride would bring her own stuff to help start things off. This bundle, called a trousseau, would include doilies, linens, lingerie, and other personal items. Over time, cash became king and a dowry was considered more important than what goods a bride could carry with her. The trousseau turned into a list of starter items that the bride and her mother were responsible for filling. Now the duty has spread to family and friends, hence the registry to help them know what to buy.

Start planning your registry at least six months prior to the wedding and complete it two months before the big day (or one month before any bridal or Couple's Shower).

A standard four-piece place setting includes a dinner fork, dinner knife, salad/dessert fork, and teaspoon. You can upgrade with a soupspoon and a butter spreader. If you want to go crazy, add serving pieces, including a meat fork, salad fork, serving spoon, gravy ladle, pie server, large butter knife, and a sugar spoon. Are your kitchen drawers exploding yet?

Be sure to send a handwritten thank-you note to every gift giver. Sending the note soon after receiving the gift is always best, and you should strive to send all thank-yous within three months of your wedding. Written acknowledgment of any gift you receive is always proper etiquette. This applies to engagement and bridal shower gifts as well.

Most guests try to give a gift that equals the cost of their (and their date's) attending the wedding. But that's only common practice, so don't get your hopes too high. Although a recent survey of newlyweds found that about 90 percent received many or most of the items they included on their registries.

IT'S YOUR WEDDING TOO!

TRY TO LOOK beyond traditional places and add a few groom-friendly items to your registry.

Home down payment. Over thirty mortgage companies nationwide participate in the FHA Bridal Registry Account. Participating mortgage companies set up an interest-bearing account and provide information on how the account works to friends and family of the couple. For more information about the program call 1-800-CALL-FHA or visit the Housing of Urban Development online (hud.gov).

Honeymoon travel. Web sites including The Big Day (thebigday.com), After I Do (afterido.com), Honey Luna (honeyluna.com), and The Honeymoon (thehoneymoon.com) allow your guests to contribute funds to all or part of your honeymoon itinerary. You might want to keep the moonlight nude mud wrap treatment off the list.

Home improvement. Both Home Depot and Lowe's have registries to fulfill your desire for gifts that build, destroy, and definitely don't belong in the kitchen.

Stocks and cash. Greenwish (greenwish.com) allows you to request contributions to stock funds or just cold hard cash.

Electronics and more. Online, it's simple to request registry items from Amazon. Offline, just go to Target or Wal-Mart and make sure all your items require batteries (and don't forget to register for batteries).

Outdoors and adventure. REI is a great place to add camping gear, his-and-her bicycles, and night-vision goggles to your wedding loot.

Home stuff. Try Target, Wal-Mart, Restoration Hardware, and Crate and Barrel. You'll have to fight for your stuff, as your fiancée might be distracted by all the blenders, cutlery, and table lamps on display.

Charity. The I Do Foundation (idofoundation.org) allows you to select from a wide variety of charities as gift alternatives.

HAVE YOU HEARD THE ONE ABOUT THE JEWISH GROOM AND CATHOLIC BRIDE?

A wedding is just like a funeral except that you get to smell your own flowers.
(Grace Hansen)

THERE'S NO WAY to make everyone happy with this wedding. It will ruffle a few family feathers. Deb and I are trying to be inclusive of all, but not too specific toward one. We're not that religious, but certain members of both our families have a vested interest in what's going to happen on our wedding day. As if that's what will condemn us to an eternity of hell. Not Deb shacking up with me. Not me eating bacon cheeseburgers on the Sabbath. Not our stealing from the blind. Just kidding. I was just making change for the bus.

I'm not too interested in fighting over, or even discussing, Deb's and my religious differences. But, Deb and I do have some fundamental differences that need to be reconciled:

Deb: spent years in Catholic schools
Me: kicked out of Hebrew school on the second day

Deb: went to a church at least once since we started dating

Me: haven't been to a temple since I lost my virginity (not lost at temple—I'm not that sacrilegious)

Deb: learned enough from friends to say a few simple Jewish prayers on Passover

Me: says "Jesus Christ" daily and twice on Sundays

Oddly enough, despite our upbringings, we work well together. Deb's beautifully-strong, down-to-earth sensibility meshes easily with my procrastinating, take-the-easiest-route-possible mentality. And we want our wedding to reflect our personalities and celebrate our differences.

But, by definition, whatever we do at the wedding will be less than ideal from a strictly Jewish or Catholic point of view. I don't need years of Hebrew school or a confirmation to understand that. Although Deb did promise to convert if she ever gives birth to twin girls (she really wants girls). This might explain the in-home sperm centrifuge we received, tagged with "From Cousin Isaac, with love. Mazel Tov." Genetic engineering aside, our religious lives will be a mix, which is fine by me. Mutts make the best dogs anyway.

"OUR KIDS CAN describe themselves as Cashews—half Catholic, half Jewish," I confide to Isaac after being admonished for leaving the tribe.

"Oy" is all he could muster.

Have I dismissed thousands of years of struggle, strife, and suffering with a lame attempt to call my future offspring a mixed nut? Oy is right.

✧

AVOIDING CONTROVERSY WAS a big reason why I wanted to elope. Deb would elope if she could still have access to her mom's wedding fund, but no such offer was extended. However you slice it, our ceremony will be taking place in a few weeks and, right now,

89

we have to put the finishing touches on something short, sweet, and hopefully memorable. In a good way.

What we're going to do and say reflects the strong sense of family and friendship we both have been exposed to. We're including a Blessing of the Hands that Deb found online. I will be breaking a glass at the end. And to round things out, we selected a female minister who has performed scores of mixed marriages. Although I doubt mixed marriages raise many eyebrows in Vegas. Maybe an interspecies union would cause a stir in Sin City? But a Jew and a Catholic? Please.

While Vegas wouldn't cast a stern eye on mixed marriages, it's a little more complicated with some families. Parents can place high expectations on their kids' weddings (not to mention his or her supposed "soulmate"). After all, if mom and dad put pressure on grades, college, and career, why stop now when there's a nuptial to knock down?

Bringing home a girlfriend from another faith might be grounds for an immediate veto regardless of how sweet she might be. But the mixing isn't always about faith. It could be social standing. Tastes in food. Dog versus cat lover. You never know what could rub a family the wrong way. And how a family reacts:

- Disowning of son.
- Writing of letters to Dear Abby or Doctor Phil on son's behalf.
- Posting online dating profiles for son.
- Calling the girlfriend of son. Constantly.
- Inviting ex-girlfriends of son to dinner. Constantly.
- Applying son to *The Bachelor*, *The Bachelorette*, and *Blind Date*.
- Performing creative brake repairs on girlfriend of son's car.

Fortunately, Deb's faring well with my parents. Although it's not hard to beat Lisa, my senior prom date, first love, and first parental pain in the ass. Lisa dressed like Madonna (*Material Girl*), Jennifer Beals (*Flashdance*), and Molly Ringwald (*Pretty in Pink*). All on the same day. She convinced me to cut school, stay out past my curfew, and rob the local 7-Eleven. Well, maybe make a large Slurpee and only pay for a medium, but I never felt so alive.

Of course, some members of both our families have expressed ceremonial issues. Luckily, we classify them not as offensive righteousness, but as defensive religiousness. Translation: religion doesn't become important until threatened. You can't use logic to argue against that one. Deb still has a hard time explaining to her Aunt Maria why we picked Vegas.

✧

"LET'S DO VEGAS," I yelled into the cell phone with nickels dropping from my slot machine. I went to a convention in Vegas a few days after I proposed.

"That's really what you want?" Deb asks.

"It's a party town. And we're party people. How could we go wrong?"

Deb took that bait and never looked back. Maybe we should have? I lost count of how many people have taken issue with our venue. Mostly we hear:

"Vegas? Really?"
"Poor Deb."
"Did you get a chapel comped or something?"
"Was Atlantic City booked?"
"Who lost that bet?"

But Las Vegas can be formal as well. Plus, it's an easy flight for most. And a great place to relax for the weekend (bride-and-groom-to-be excluded). Of course, you can't avoid the cheese factor. You just have to embrace it and spread it evenly to avoid any nasty buildup. We spent a weekend in Vegas scouting out places. It was ironic to have planning meetings at places like the Four Seasons while we were staying at the cheapest place I could book online: the Westward Ho motel. The Ho, as locals like to call it, is home to the 99-cent pound hotdog, which—trust me—is not for the faint of heart. Especially when you have two pounds' worth as back-to-back meals.

In Vegas, literally anyone can marry you. Merlin could have performed the ceremony. I would have to slay a dragon before completing our vows amongst a gang of pixies as witnesses. That's the MGM Grand. You can also get married atop the Eiffel Tower at the Paris Casino. Or in a replica of Studio 54. Seventies clothes included. And don't forget the drive-thru services up and down the Strip.

A lot of Vegas weddings are spur-of-the-moment or just involve a few people. We, bucking the trend, are planning on a nice formal affair.

Our last stop was a resort, thirty miles off the Strip. Immediately, we knew this was it. The Hyatt Lake Las Vegas had an amazing deck overlooking a lake and more than enough room for an outdoor ceremony. And to top it off, we were told Julia Roberts, John Cusack, Catherine Zeta-Jones, and Billy Crystal graced the resort while filming *America's Sweethearts*. The fact that the whole movie takes place at the Hyatt seemed like a good enough omen to cinch the deal. Okay, it was at least something positive to cling to in a land of sleaze, neon, and overindulgence.

✧

"HELLO? WHO SHOULD say what?" Deb inquires. "A little help, please."

I have to find two ceremony readings and decide who should read them. That would be an all-day activity unless Deb already provided me with a few options. I keep my "eenie, meenie, minie, moe" decision-making silent and officially decree *The Velveteen Rabbit* (by Margery Williams) for my cousin Allyson and "Friendship" (by Judy Bielicki) for my friend Brent. I feel guilty for missing Brent's wedding. You don't realize how important some things are until you go through them yourself, so I want to offer something special to him. I am sure he'd be happier with one hundred dollars in casino chips, but he's got the gift of gab. And gab at my wedding he will.

Deb's not too pleased with how our ceremony talk is going today. To raise our spirits, we watch *America's Sweethearts* for the sixth time. We are thinking of having it play on our wedding shuttle bus. As the movie starts, I begin to savor a rare ninety minutes of quiet time. Quiet, except for the poking and prodding Deb does when the resort shows up on screen.

Deb's movie comments include:

"Are we getting those chairs?"
"Will our food look that good?"
"I like those place settings."
"Look at the view. That's our view."

My movie thoughts include:

"Will I have time to gamble before or after we cut the cake?"
"Julia looks good."
"Why can't I be in a movie?"
"How lucky is John Cusack?"

The entire meteorologist community and I are ready to guarantee that Las Vegas has a zero percent chance of rainfall during our entire wedding month.

I quote the Internet. "In October one can expect an average high of eighty-two degrees and an average low of fifty-four. Las Vegas averages two hundred and ninety-four days of sunshine per year. Two hundred and eleven perfectly clear days and eighty-three partly cloudy ones."

But this isn't good enough for Deb. We have to order rain insurance. I let this charge go through without the usual money fight. It was cheap, and stranger things have happened. After all, we should hedge against any acts of God. Either God.

Deb sleeps easier. I lie awake wondering what my life would be like if I had married Lisa, my senior prom date. What would she look like now? Would she still have railroad-track braces, leg warmers, and an insatiable thirst for wine coolers? I still have a thing for leg warmers. I'll save that little bit of perversion for when it really might come in handy, like a potential seven-year itch with Deb.

I DO.
NOW GIMME BACK THE DAMN DICE!
VEGAS WEDDING FACTS:

LAS VEGAS IS the most popular U.S. wedding destination, and, like the casinos, the chapels keep raking the couples in.

Marriage license applications issued in Clark County, NV (Las Vegas)

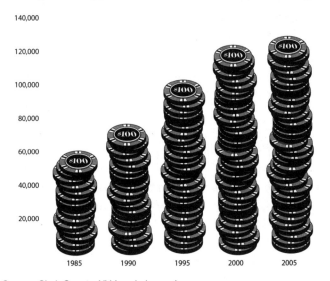

Source: Clark County, NV (co.clark.nv.us)

The only city that beats Vegas is Istanbul, Turkey, with 166,000 ceremonies each year.

Source: Association for Wedding Professionals International (afwpi.com)

YOU'RE JEWISH. SHE'S CATHOLIC?
YOU'RE HINDU. SHE'S PROTESTANT?
YOU'RE TEXAN. SHE'S CALIFORNIAN?

IN 2005, 16 percent of U.S. weddings have multifaith or multi-cultural ceremonies. Are you in one of them?
Source: 2005 American Wedding Study, The Fairchild Bridal Group

Here are a few suggestions on handling interfaith weddings:
- Mix it up. Have two officiants to represent each of your faiths.
- Relief religion. Find someone from a third religion (e.g., Unitarian Church) who might be more open to interfaith ceremonies.
- Eenie meenie. Choose one faith and go all in.
- Double up. Have two separate ceremonies.
- Be civil. Skip the religion part altogether and have a judge (or ship captain) do the honors.
- Start anew. Ask a friend or relative to become an ordained minister. Since you'll be in on the ground floor, there will be no pesky thousand-year-old traditions getting in your way.

Some tips to help ease the tensions:
- Plan ahead.
- Discuss often.
- Interview officiants. Expect them to interview you, too.
- Share with family. But remember, ultimately it's your day.

Remember, it doesn't stop at the "I do's." Things you should also discuss before the big day:
- What holidays will you celebrate?
- What place(s) of worship will you attend?
- How does religion factor into your daily life?
- How does religion factor into your extended families?
- What about when you have kids (e.g., circumcision, christening, churches or synagogues, religious schools, parenting styles, bringing up in both faiths)?

JUKE BOX
HERO.

What counts in making a happy marriage is not so much how compatible you are, but how you deal with incompatibility.
(George Levinger)

I HAVEN'T SOUGHT much counsel from friends and family about the wedding and my involvement, but I should get some feedback from someone other than Deb. Where should I start? After all, I've done pretty well for myself during the past thirty years. I survived a public high school filled with nine hundred and ninety-nine kids cooler than me, got my own jobs, placed in the 99th percentile on the SAT and GMAT (hence why everyone else was cooler than me), stayed clear of jail, and even found a bride. I score myself a six hundred in the batting average of life. That's a pre-engagement statistic. Post-engagement, it's more like a fifty. Not fifty-fifty. Just fifty. Five zero. One in twenty. Fortunately, the engagement ring has been keeping my player contract alive. I need help. But who should I ask? I'm the first of my cohorts to take the marriage plunge.

I have always looked up to my Uncle Bob. He's only ten years older than me, which has made him more like an older brother than an uncle. Growing up, I spent a lot of time with Bob, whether he liked it or not. It was Bob who took me skiing. Let me hang out with his lifeguard buddies. Taught me how to drive. He even let me shoot Jesus with his BB gun.

✧

I WAS FOURTEEN. Bob was excited to have bought a BB gun. We went straight to his room and started shooting whatever was in sight. Bullets were bouncing everywhere. Finally, our attention focused on a laminated picture of Jesus that Bob used for work. Bob sold laminating equipment, and churches were a big customer. I only wish I were wise enough then to know how valuable access to a photo ID machine would be. Many of my social awkwardness might have been eliminated if I starting bar-hopping at fourteen. Of course, that might have negatively impacted my standardized test scores, but I think it would have been worth it.

The first to shoot Jesus square in the eyes won. Well, Jesus had the last laugh. On my first try, the BB missed altogether and struck a nearby lighter, which started to uncontrollably fizz. We panicked, and the next thing I remember is the toilet overflowing after us jamming the lighter and a roll of toilet paper into the bowl. Moral of this story: don't mess with Jesus, my marrying a Catholic girl notwithstanding.

✧

"HOW SHOULD I deal with all this preparation?" I ask Bob, desperate for some wisdom beyond my years. And hopefully beyond his as well.

"Just go with the flow." Either Bob's way deep. Or so not deep.

"I thought I was doing that by letting Deb be in charge. But it's proven to be more pain than pleasure."

"That's a wedding. Hell, that was my wedding. Good luck. Speaking of luck, see you in Vegas." Okay, so he's so not deep. But still, it's some form of advice.

Go with the flow? No, I had to *be* the Flow. In fact, tonight, Deb's going to meet the Flow. During the whole ride home from work I bustle with energy. I am going to make her proud today.

Either that or fall straight to sleep, crashing from the five Cokes I just downed. After all, I needed fuel to kick-start the Flow.

✧

FIRST TASK FOR the Flow: table planning. A great place to make my mark. I lead Deb straight to the home whiteboard. We are expecting a hundred guests.

"How should I arrange them?" Deb asks in a rhetorical sort of way.

"The families are easy. Lump them together." Ta da.

"And our friends, Mr. Flow?" she asks. Such a nonbeliever.

"Group by relationship status. Put the Cs (Couples) together. Pair WSMs (Woman Seeking Man) with MSWs (Man Seeking Woman). And we must keep any MSMWS (Man Seeking Meaningless Wedding Sex) far away from our vulnerable WSMVB (Woman Seeking Marriage Very Badly)."

"We really do have to get her married."

"First things first. We need to get us married."

We debate the merits of a large head table versus a private love-table. Social seating or sweetheart seclusion? Constant chatter or controlled conversation? Scattered stares or serious scrutiny?

I am thinking too long on this one. I must react. "Head table!" I bellow.

"Fair enough." Deb seems pleased.

Table planning done. Score one for the Flow. I compliment myself on my spatial abilities. A feeling of gleeful bliss takes over and warms my heart.

Task number two: the music list.

Bliss over.

✧

PICKING THE BAND was like the registry, give and take. I gave and Deb took. Besides the bachelor party and a big-screen television, my other main priority was to make sure the band was cool.

My two top band picks were Dave Wakeling and the Cheeseballs. Dave Wakeling, formerly of English Beat, played the night Deb and I got engaged. The Cheeseballs are an awesome San

Francisco eighties cover band. And who doesn't like the eighties? That would be my preferred wedding atmosphere, rocking to the music of my high school days. Take that, all you girls who wouldn't dance with me.

Deb preferred a little more range. Say a few more decades. But she agreed to consider my picks. As always, she's the embracing one. Unfortunately, both bands are way too expensive, especially since we have to fly them to Vegas. A smidge over our band budget. Actually a smidge over our total wedding budget. Guess Deb knew this beforehand.

During our reception-scouting trip to Vegas, we spoke to a local talent agent. I gave him a simple and surprisingly well-understood requirement. "We want the Cheeseballs of Vegas."

"That would be Modern Love."

We saw them, and they really were the Cheeseballs of Vegas. What more could you ask for? According to Deb, who was now faced with a reasonable band bill, "something more family-friendly." We agreed Modern Love would overpower the reception (read: upstage the bride), and picked a subtler, more general (read: more generic) band lead by the wife of the talent agent. No nepotism there. And, unfortunately, no family discount. I guess I have to wait to chaperone our kids' dance to rock out to Twisted Sister.

✧

Thanks to the Internet and the Billboard Top 100 charts, we're pleasantly surprised at how easy it is for us to choose songs we both like. We start with a healthy sampling of the eighties ("All Night Long," "Come on Eileen," "Love Shack") and headed down to the seventies ("Dancing Queen," "That's the Way I Like It," "Brick House"), even further down ("Steppin' Out With My Baby," "A Fine Romance," "Dancing Cheek to Cheek"), and back up to present day ("Shake Your Bon Bon," "Oops! . . . I Did It Again," "Get This Party Started"). Along the way, we sprinkle in a good bit of Latin salsa music for Deb's contingency (Deb's half Puerto Rican and half Irish, which makes for quite a potent mix, especially when I do something wrong). My hips begin to hurt already. Even with all those break-dancing lessons I took in junior high.

We schedule time for the *hora*. And I trade the electric slide for the chicken dance. I hate both, but I consider the chicken dance the lesser of two evils.

But before any of these songs would play, I knew that our first dance could be my complete undoing. The mental image of me dancing in front of everyone becomes my silent dread for the remainder of the night.

As I sit on the couch, I try tapping my feet to the beat of commercial jingles, seeing if there's any rhythm in me. Nope, but now I can't stop wishing I was an Oscar Mayer wiener. How apropos.

AFTER AN ETERNITY of mental anguish (Now, if I really were an Oscar Mayer wiener, would everyone be in love with me? It can't be that simple, can it?), I finally fall asleep.

But not for long. I wake up in a cold sweat, yelling, "Stop looking. I am not a wiener. I am just a white man with no beat!"

YOUR FIRST DANCE SONG

BUT, WHAT ABOUT Metallica?

According to *Mobile Beat Magazine,* the top twenty-five bridal songs for 2005 were:

Rank	Song	Artist
1	Amazed	Lonestar
2	From This Moment On	Shania Twain and Bryan White
3	Wonderful Tonight	Eric Clapton
4	It's Your Love	Tim McGravy and Faith Hill
5	At Last	Etta James
6	What a Wonderful World	Louis Armstrong
7	Unchained Melody	Righteous Brothers
8	Unforgettable	Natalie and Nat King Cole

9	Can't Help Falling in Love	Elvis Presley
10	Have I Told You Lately	Rod Stewart / Van Morrison
11	The Way You Look Tonight	Frank Sinatra
12	I Cross My Heart	George Strait
13	All My Life	K-Ci & JoJo
14	Could I Have This Dance	Anne Murray
15	I Do (Cherish You)	98 Degrees
16	Hero	Enrique Iglesias
17	I Swear	John M. Montgomery / All 4 One
18	I Hope You Dance	Lee Ann Womack
19	A Moment Like This	Kelly Clarkson
20	Beautiful	Christina Aguilera
21	(Everything I Do) I Do It For You	Bryan Adams
22	I Don't Want to Miss a Thing	Aerosmith
23	Because You Loved Me	Celine Dion
24	Truly Madly Deeply	Savage Garden
25	Keeper of the Stars	Tracy Byrd

Source: *Mobile Beat Magazine* (mobilebeat.com/top200.asp)

Three minutes down, only three hours of music to go.

If you thought the eighties were the only decade that mattered musically, good for you. Even if it is your big day, think of your guests. Some of whom may be in their eighties. Mix your music up a bit. Include slow, fast, couple-friendly, group, and, yes, eighties songs.

IS YOUR WEDDING SHAPING UP TO BE HATFIELD VS. MCCOY II? HOW TO SEAT PEOPLE.

Lay it down. You should first sort guests by category (e.g., family, work, college, and hometown). Write down information for each person that might be handy when deciding who sits where.

Start at the top. Decide who will sit with you and your bride. There are endless variations to how your table is arranged, from just the two of you to you, your bride, the parents, best man, and maid of honor, to the whole wedding party. Pick an arrangement that suits your desires and fits the room. You may want to spread members of the wedding party around to "host" tables. You should also place close family and friends nearest to your table.

Mix it up. Don't just seat people together because they know one another. There will plenty of time to chat at the bar. Arrange folks to spark conversation, romance, and business deals. Be sure to get a cut of whatever may result.

Keep it safe. Don't seat people with axes to grind or grudges to hold together. Also, be kind to your elders. Make sure they are away from loud speakers and have ample room to move around.

Fill it out. Don't have one table only half-full. Spread the space among all tables.

Let them know. Have printed table cards available in a convenient place during the cocktail hour or entryway to the reception hall. A map and alphabetical listing of guests with their table numbers is also helpful. Instead of plain table numbers, you may want to label tables with fun names (e.g., vacation spots you and your fiancée have gone, cities you have lived in, hobbies you enjoy, poets who best express your feelings).

SHE MAY NOT REMEMBER TO BACK UP HER COMPUTER, BUT SHE KNOWS TO BACK UP HER WEDDING DRESS.

Politics doesn't make strange bedfellows.
Marriage does.
(Groucho Marx)

A BUSINESS DAYTRIP to Los Angeles. It's nice to get out of the office. But even better to get out of cell coverage (read: wedding coverage) from Deb. I know they have cell phones in L.A., but that's my story and I am sticking to it. Maybe Verizon should offer a wedding planning plan: unlimited fiancée-to-fiancé minutes during their wedding planning and about ten free minutes a month for the next twenty years of marriage.

As all couples gradually do, I am becoming more and more like Deb. Case in point: my flight anxiety. In between prayers to my God, I think about Deb's God. Are they different? What about our kids? Would it be easier if I married a Jew? Did I ever really date a Jew? It only really happened once. Not sure why. Was it that I left New York too quickly?

Was I subconsciously rebelling against my family? Do Jews not find me attractive? Does any faith find me attractive?

MY ONE JEWISH date wasn't my finest moment. I responded to her personal ad in the weekly town paper. And what an ad. "Gorgeous, athletic, beautiful blond seeking tall guy with big feet. Call with name, number, and shoe size."

It was my roommate who brought the ad to my attention. While I was not one to troll the personal sections, except to get the occasional thrill reading "women seeking woman" postings, he was a big fan. He successfully created six different personas and started dating like it was going out of style. Who am I kidding? The acts of a desperate man seeking sex any way possible never goes out of style. We had to get a second phone line installed as I struggled to keep up with the comings and goings of Steve, Joe, Chris, Chris, Dave, and John. It's too bad they all weren't splitting the rent with me.

"Craig, if you answer just one ad, this is it," my roommate said.

He was right. I had to make the call.

"Hi. I'm Craig and I really liked your personal ad. You know I don't really read personals, not that there's anything wrong with personals. It's just that I, well, my roommate, well, I saw your ad and it was very interesting. I mean the most I get for having a size fourteen shoe is usually pain and suffering at Athlete's Foot. Wait. I don't have athlete's foot, I just shop there. Not too successfully, because of my big feet. Anyway. Yup. Craig. Size fourteen. Call me. Thanks."

She called. And since I had the biggest feet of all her respondents, I got the date. It was pleasant enough. Yes, she was quite fetching, but weird. Probably not weird on the California granola scale, but she broke the bizarre scale of this Long Island meat-and-potato kid.

I overlooked her weaker points (read: her interest in everything organic and crystal) and searched for her inner beauty (read: how she looked in a tight sweater) and asked for date number two. My suaveness during date number one obviously made an impression on her. When I picked her up for date number two, she had a gift for me. Wow, it's usually the other way around. I was so excited.

"Open it now. It'll be great for you."

This is awesome. She's not crazy; she's cool. Someone this thoughtful could be the woman of my dreams.

"Come on, already. It'll be great for us." For us? Reserve the temple. Call my mom. No, call my mom and then reserve the temple.

I open the package. "Spirolina?" What do I do with this? What is this powder? Is it a passion food? An aphrodisiac? Hopefully I'll be licking it off her body later.

"It cleanses your spirit. Just a spoonful a day. Mix it in anything, as long as it's not animal-based."

"You shouldn't have."

At dinner, I had a spinach salad. I wasn't going to risk losing the opportunity for my size-fourteen feet to commingle under the sheets with hers (only a size seven, but I can live with that) by revealing my ugly carnivore side just yet. She had lettuce and tofu scramble for dinner. Halfway through dinner, I was still trying to figure out what my spirit did to deserve the spirolina. And my date's body must have been trying to figure out why it never digests a hearty steak. She fell ill (does tofu go bad?) and had to cut dinner short. I left the date hungry. At home, I made a protein shake (must have protein) and added the spirolina for kicks. I threw up and kept clear of personals—and spirolina—ever since.

BEING A COMPANY man, I resist answering Deb's calls during our L.A. meeting. Apparently voice mail isn't immediate enough.

"GR8 411. GOT WED DRESS FOR $50," Deb texts me.

A text message? Cool. Did she finally read her phone's manual? Did the dress salesperson (who, after selling Deb a fifty-dollar dress, is now my best friend) help? Am I not giving Deb enough technology credit? Is this how other great female scientific breakthroughs happened? A woman just needing to connect more with her man? Was Madame Curie X-ray research meant to improve worldkind? Or was she just suspicious about her husband's locked briefcase?

A fifty-dollar dress? Awesome. This good news warrants violating any communications embargo. "R U GOING 2 RETURN $3K DRESS?" I joyously thumb type.

"4 BACKUP ONLY. IF U THINK I AM GIVING UP DRESS 1, U CRAZY." Her reply actually arrives before I pressed SEND on my phone. She knows me too well.

I DON'T SAY much at the meetings. I miss Deb. But even more important, I miss having more time to plan a honeymoon that's two weeks away. I must book something fast.

On the flight home, I devour way too many snacks. I try to resist, but the power of a family-size bag of Oreos I picked up at the airport is too strong. After my twentieth, I feel regret. Who's got time to hit the gym? Deb's big on trying Internet diets. At least a half-dozen times this year, boxes would arrive from places far and wide, filled with mysterious fluids, powders, and pills (thankfully, no spirolina) of promises. Alas, no magic elixir to report. I am grateful my rented tux pants possess an adjustable zipper track along the waist.

"AND WHERE WILL we be going?" Deb asks at the airport.

"Home, I thought. Unless you're having a seedy rent a room at the airport motel moment?"

"Where are we going on our honeymoon? Focus."

"I swear it'll be done tonight. I was thinking about it all day."

I remind myself to avoid car trips with Deb at all costs for the next two weeks. Too much potential for uninterrupted talk time. Although it really only takes a second to put me in my place.

After Deb goes to bed, I dig into some honeymoon planning or dig myself out of honeymoon planning, depending on your perspective. And I actually finish it all. Hawaii is so cliché, but time is running out and it seems like the safest exotic place given current political climates. A simple plan: pick an island, buy a guidebook, and park our butts there for two weeks.

Mission accomplished. Kauai, Hawaii. The resort has free mai tai happy hours (but now that I think about it, don't most?) and, most important, vacancies. This is too easy. Should I wait longer for an once-in-a-lifetime deal that could pop up the week before our wedding? But if it doesn't, the back-of-the-bus tour of Central America that's left might result in a forever-lifetime of pain. Way beyond the cheap-bus, bouncy-seat pain.

To top off my accomplishment, I order a copy of *The Ultimate Kauai Guidebook* gift-wrapped and FedExed to Deb.

Feeling good, I slip into bed, hoping for some loving for all my hard work. Mission impossible. All I get is a grunt from Deb, a tissue box, and a finger pointed toward the bottle of moisturizer on her nightstand. A foreshadowing moment, if I ever felt one.

OH, I'LL TAKE YOU SOMEWHERE. "TO THE MOON, ALICE!"

TAKING A HONEYMOON has its roots in the ancient days of bride capture. Once a man snagged his woman, they needed to get away for a while to allow family emotions to calm back down. Then when the couple returned, everyone would be ready to accept the marriage. You're probably not using your honeymoon to escape her family . . . yet. But regardless, some R&R after the I Do's is probably in order.

The average honeymoon lasts eight days and costs $3,700, including transportation, lodging, meals, and all those great sightseeing tours.

Source: money.cnn.com/2005/06/08/pf/best_honeymoons

On your trip, be sure to tell everyone you are on your honeymoon. You might get bumped or upgraded. Also, if you have room in your suitcase, bring extra wedding favors as thank-yous for the people who go out of their way to help. Of course, a bigger tip might be preferred, but one of your favors is a nice gesture.

To guarantee she's in the mood, preorder champagne and a fruit basket for your arrival.

Want to be one of the crowd? Here are the 2005 most popular honeymoon cities:

Paris	San Francisco
Venice	Sydney
Honolulu	

Want to go where the pros suggest? Here are the top overall destinations from a survey of over six thousand travel agents:

Hawaii	St. Lucia
Italy	Mexico
Tahiti	St. Barth's
Anguilla	Jamaica
Fiji	France

Want to be a trendsetter? Here are some up and coming honeymoon suggestions from *Modern Bride*:

Costa Rica	Fiji
South Africa	Vietnam
Belize	Anguilla
Turks & Caicos	Dominican Republic
New Zealand	Australia

Source: modernbride.com/travel/top50

Already thinking about where to consummate your marriage? After the bed, the top three places for honeymoon sex are:

1. Shower
2. Hot tub
3. Balcony

Source: "A Nice Ring to It," *Men's Health,* June 2002

Packing tips:
- Go light.
- Bring a copy of marriage certificate (might be necessary in case the airline tickets don't match your wife's driver's license or passport).
- Use credit cards and traveler's checks, not cash.
- Include extra film or camera memory, and batteries.
- Pack for fun and adventure.
- Remember protection (both the SPF and anti-parenthood kind).

Traveling out of country?

Go to the State Department's Web site (travel.state.gov) for information on passport and visa information and any travel warnings. It's also a good idea to check the Center for Disease Control's Web site (cdc.gov/travel) for any health (or lack thereof) information about your dream destination.

ANALYZE ME AND I'LL PUT YOUR KIDS THROUGH HARVARD.

Marriage is a great institution,
but I'm not ready for an institution.
(Mae West)

"SO, I'M CURED, right?" I ask Dr. McMahon, my therapist.

This hasn't been a long-term counseling project—more like a quick sanity check. The five free sessions, courtesy of my health insurance, are utterly useless. Who would ever declare me sane?

I saw a therapist once before, when I was trying to muster the nerve to break up with someone. Too bad we were living together already. I sucked at breaking up, so why not let a professional be the bad guy? No dice. Where are the unethical quacks willing to diagnose me as a bona fide wimp after one session and call my girlfriend on my behalf? It took another year before that relationship ended, and it wasn't therapy that moved it along—it was a cross-country work relocation I forgot to mention to her. And even then it took a few months of dime-a-minute, three-thousand-mile, painful conversations to really end the relationship.

The need for breakup support is well behind me. I have never felt the love I have for Deb. But love isn't the issue. It's the rest of my life that needs an overhaul.

"I worry. I always do."

"Go on."

"I wanted to start marriage on the right foot."

"And that means?"

"Everyone is happy."

"Why does everyone need to be happy?"

"Everyone has their differences."

"Define differences."

"Noun. The state of being different."

"What's different about you?"

"Besides my bedwetting?"

"Now you're talking."

DEB AND I didn't do any pre-wedding couples counseling. Maybe that would have helped relieve the anxiety we're feeling. Okay, the anxiety I'm feeling. Some couples swear by it ("I really didn't know who I was about to marry until I sat down and spent two days asking him every question I could think of, but was too lazy to ask over the eight years of us dating," one of Deb's friends confided), but it is too late. Plus, I have had enough "so how does that make you feel?" recently.

My final diagnosis is nothing new to me, but even so, I might have lost something in the translation.

> **What my therapist says:** "It's all right to worry. And it's possible to stop worrying about everything, but that has to come from within."
> **What I hear:** "Get some balls and stop making your company pay for these bitch sessions." Or is it "Get some balls and stop making your company pay for these sessions, bitch."

I'll have to wait until my next insurance plan year to pick this up.

✧

DEB AND I venture out with some friends. Deb loves going out. But lately, I haven't been much of a partier. At least when Deb's out with me. I can't stop seeing everything through the lens of marriage. Deb's talking to some random guy at the bar. What's that about? What does he have that I don't? Does he drive a fancier car? Does Deb even care about that? I would like to drive a fancier car, but can't justify the expense with a family to save for. Does Deb appreciate that? Can the guy she just touched give her both the fancy car and the savings account? Okay, maybe she didn't touch on purpose, but contact is contact (except this time, Deb's not figuring out this guy's ring size—like my *contact* at Tiffany's). Does Deb still want to marry me? Why do all the women look so hot tonight? Is it just because I'm unavailable? Is it too late to re-up the therapy? Maybe I should change jobs to get another five free therapy sessions right away?

As my friends chatter away, asking about the wedding, I struggle to reach a mental happy place. What about how I met Deb? It was a totally different experience than how I met anyone else, and as such, reinforces why we are destined to be together. Ahh, happy place.

✧

IT WAS THE one time I tried to be Mr. Cool. We happened to be on the same flight. On the jetway to the plane, Deb innocently broke the ice.

"I can't believe how early this flight is. This is great."

I was still reeling from running halfway through SFO, and, as such, wasn't in any mood for conversation. But I felt a spark. She was pretty. Like a traveler who can fly for twenty hours straight and still look put together. My outfit was totally wrinkled, thanks to waking up late from a nap and rushing out the door to catch my plane. The cattle call of fellow Southwest Airlines passengers didn't give me time to think about what was actually happening.

By the time I got to my middle, last row seat, I realized I had missed a perfect opportunity to be engaging (no pun intended) with Deb. I stewed in that nonreclining seat with no armrest access throughout the entire flight. When we landed, Deb was nowhere in sight. And neither was my luggage. Forty-five minutes later, still no bag. But, Deb approached. Second chance, here I come.

"Um, hi again. Do you know where our bags are?" she politely asked.

"Well, if you didn't jinx us on the way down, they'd be here by now." Smooth, Craig. Smooth.

Luckily, Deb could take a joke. And that's why I had to see her again. We were working the same trade show. Since I knew where she'd be all week, I decided to avoid looking too desperate by asking for her number right then. Of course, when the show opened, I frantically searched for her booth. And after a few playful minutes of chitchat, I looked really cool when I walked away, telling Deb to stop by my booth sometime. After all, I could always return for another one of her informative (What did her company do again? I was too busy looking at her to listen.) product demonstrations. How romantic.

Deb never came by. And after two days of no contact, thinking about her between handing out company brochures, I reverted to Mr. Uncool. Welcome back, old friend. I staked out her booth for hours. No luck.

For most of us, this would be the end of the story. Two ships passing in the night. But I was just getting warmed up. I searched my alumni directories for someone who worked at Deb's company and I begged him for her number ("Yup, they're teaching groveling now at our school. It's a core class."). While it would be easier for me just to call the company operator, the truth was that I didn't remember her last name and I didn't want to ask for a "pretty brunette named Deb, I think." Nick, my newfound alumni friend, turned out to know Deb but wasn't comfortable giving out her info. After a few days of constant petitioning ("Yup, pleading is now an elective"), Nick finally relented. I called Deb. She said that she did stop by to see me and left a message, which I never received. We laughed about my attempt at coolness (always good to make fun of oneself; little did she know what she was getting herself into) and planned for an actual, nonprofessional date.

Our first date went well. Dinner, drinks, and conversation for hours. I was worried that things might go south after Deb informed me that the last time she sat at this table of the restaurant I picked, her boyfriend broke up with her. But a few of my charming stories seem to make Deb's post-breakup two weeks of tears, phone-calling, and hanging up fade away.

" . . . and then I got a Mickey Mouse drum set for being potty trained." I was still smooth.

Our second date was a dinner and movie and ended with a private Scrabble session. Why I wasn't scooped up earlier is beyond comprehension. We did some serious betting that night. She got a back rub, and I got seven minutes in the closet. Not as in the sixteen-year-old, Seven Minutes in Heaven version. More as in the four-year-old take-a-time-out-for-being-a-bit-too-fresh with the back rubbing.

During our third date, Deb half-jokingly asked me to join her on a trip to Costa Rica the following week. To her surprise, I all-seriously agreed. That might have sent other women running for the hills, but Deb took it in stride. What a catch.

Our fourth date was spent tropical-clothes shopping.

And the fifth was back at SFO, on our way to Costa Rica. We had a blast. While we were head-over-heels for each other before we left on the trip, spending the week together sealed the deal. Or, as I rhetorically asked before jumping into our private hot tub, "There's no going back, is there?"

DEB AND I are meant to be together. I love her with all my heart. But of course, I worry. I worry about all those former girlfriends that got away. Do they still pine for me? Were we better matched? A quick stroll down memory lane provides all the answers I need:

I got dumped in Sears by my junior prom date (she of the baby-blue-matching-cummerbund dress and not-quite-gold-bracelet) the day after the prom. I went to see her at work and then had to ride my bike a long five miles home, tears dripping down my face the whole trip back.

I met a girl that wore a hat like the children's book character Paddington Bear. To impress her I bought a huge Paddington Bear and put it in a box in front of her house. True to the bear story, I attached a note about how the bear was lost and needed her to help find his owner (that would be me) and would probably get a thank-you dinner if she called. I couldn't wait for her to call, so I coincidentally Rollerbladed by her house and stuck to the story as she opened the door. Of course I didn't have enough time to skate away when I saw the two guys in her house.

"Oh. What are you doing here?" the Paddington Bear girl asked.

"I lost my bear, did you see it?"

"What?"

Thankfully, her roommate stepped in. "There's a box for you over here."

Everyone looked at the bear and started to laugh. And not in a good way. Before anything else was said, I tried to leave the house still in full Rollerblade pads and helmet. The pathetic looks searing into the back of my head caused me to trip, take out a lamp, and chip a tooth. I never got the call back, but I sent her the dental bill.

A coworker who tried to seduce me on a business trip. Of course, she was drunk and I wasn't interested. So she yelled at the top of her lungs at the restaurant.

"You're picky with your clothes. Picky with your food. And obviously picky with your women."

How wrong she was. I'll wear almost anything.

A really hot girl. So hot that she had to tell me all about how she caught someone driving really close to her with his pants unzipped, pleasuring himself.

"Oh, that was you?" I innocently inquired.

Date over. While hotter than the sun, she had a very cold sense of humor.

✧

DEB AND I finish the evening with me asking too many questions about our future and ruining her night out.

"For the last time, I'll love you forever," Deb painfully replies.

"I just need a bit of reassurance. We're taking a big step soon." Hopefully, my night on the couch will reassure me.

WANT TO KNOW THE CUT OF A WOMAN? LOOK AT THE CUT OF HER DIAMOND.

ROUND

Family-centered, dependable, and nonaggressive. Round is the most popular cut, but those who wear it are often accused of lacking spontaneity.

OVAL

Individualistic, creative, and willing to take chances. An oval wearer is similar to the round wearer, but wants to be a little different. She is dependable, but willing to go crazy once in a while. Ovals aren't highly popular cuts because they can yield diamonds with poor brilliancy.

HEART

Sentimental, feminine, and trusting. Also called the "Black Widow" and the "Three Strikes" diamond as it produces the second highest divorce rate. Heart wearers are extreme romantics. And when they figure out that things aren't perfect with their mates, they often leave.

RECTANGLE
(Emerald)

Disciplined, conservative, and efficient. Rectangle wearers are also old-fashioned, but don't believe in being one of the masses. They are leaders and are attracted to this cut for its quiet elegance, regal temperament, and bold strokes.

SQUARE
(Princess)

Fun, exciting, and cutting-edge. Square wearers seek adventure. Since Square and Radiant (square with rounded edges) cuts yield the most sparkly stones, these women tend to enjoy the attention their rings generate.

PEAR

Vivacious, sociable, and demanding. Pear wearers want to be different and create a scene. However, this comes at a cost, as they tend to be a higher-maintenance group of women. Pear wearers are the third most likely to get a divorce.

MARQUISE

Extroverted, aggressive, and career-centered. The Marquise cut makes the diamond look bigger than it is. Many Marquise wearers believe that first impressions are everything and size matters. They try hard to be something they are not, which contributes to the Marquise being the number one divorce cut.

Source: *How to Buy a Diamond,* Appendix E, p. 309, Fred Cuellar, Diamond Cutters International (diamondcuttersintl.com)

ARE YOU SANE?
SHOULD YOU GET MARRIED?
DON'T WANT TO LIE ON A COUCH
AND STARE AT AN INK STAIN?

DO-IT-YOURSELF therapy questions to get you through your anxiety attacks:

- Do you think she should do better?
- Do you think you can do better?
- Look at yourself in the mirror. Do you really think you can do better?
- Can you distinguish between the role of your mother and your wife?
- Do you have dreams or nightmares more?
- Have you kept a plant alive for more than a week?
- Do you drink to escape?
- Do you escape to drink?
- How well do you handle pain?
- Are there any secrets that you still keep from your fiancée? How well can you lie?
- How well have you handled wedding questions?
- Have you cut your umbilical cord? Or are you waiting for your fiancée to do that?
- Are you comfortable with your sexuality? Is your fiancée? Besides the really kinky stuff . . . give it time.
- Are you able to give up your individuality for the greater couplehood?
- Are you a dog or cat person? What about your fiancée? Can you live with that?
- Don't you think you should go to an actual therapist and not rely on this book?

Just like the real thing, there are no right or wrong answers. But to be safe, don't share results with your fiancée. That's very wrong.

WHERE'S A CRYSTAL BALL WHEN YOU NEED ONE?

Wives are people who feel they don't dance enough.
(Groucho Marx)

I FAINTLY SEE "Time is running out!" in the specks in our bedroom ceiling. It's like a bad three-dimensional art poster telling me my fortune. Yes, time is running out. Opportunities are closing. Windows are sealing. My family doesn't understand me. I don't understand Deb's family. My single friends have written me off. Deb's married friends haven't approved me yet. I still haven't done anything truly groomworthy.

Now the ceiling is telling me to calm down. But it's too late. My heartbeat makes Deb nervous. She's now stirring, which makes me nervous. It's barely five in the morning. I head to the living room, taking solace in the Sunday *Times*. And purposely skipping the Styles section. Those rich-couple, charmed-life love stories littering the wedding announcements are a tough read this early, especially on an empty stomach. But like a horrible car wreck on the highway of life, I cannot resist taking a peek at who's married this week. My eyes widen. My mouth opens. My head slumps. Picture-perfect lives with blue-blooded families and fancy affairs. Doctors. Lawyers. Brokers. A son of a judge. A daughter of the Revolutionary War. A descendent of the Mayflower. An heir to a cha-jillion dollar fortune. Yuck.

I circle the grooms whose ass I can probably kick. Only three this week. Damn.

So, I'm a lover, not a fighter. I introduce the Styles section to our paper shredder before Deb wakes up. She, too, can't resist reading. And comparing.

Back on the couch, I go over my list of to-do's. Too much, too early. I need food. I need distractions. Three bagels and six episodes of *The Simpsons* later, I calm down. Bless you TiVo.

✧

"TODAY'S THE DAY!" Deb declares as she shuts off the TV.

A sexual proclamation if I ever heard one. I start stripping.

"Hold on, hot shot. Don't even go there. We've got work to do."

"Call it whatever you want," I offer. "Sex. Work. Sex. Beggars can't be choosers."

"Well, I choose wedding work."

Not only do I put on my clothes, I frantically lace up my Nikes.

"And don't even think about running . . ."

I should have brewed coffee before Deb woke up. Its smell soothes her. But, I am face-to-face with raw, uncaffeinated Deb. To quote the wise sage I've spent my morning with thus far, "D'oh."

"You've left me no choice. We're going to crash talk about whatever's left to crash talk about," Deb demands.

It's clear that showing up to the wedding isn't enough. My opinion matters. That's sweet. Time to give Deb my undivided attention. She deserves it. Plus, there aren't any more *Simpsons* episodes recorded. But really, it's because Deb took the batteries out of the remote control and threw them out the window.

If men were told that bad behavior in their present life would result in an ever-repeating, never-getting-it-right, wedding-planning afterlife, I am positive the world would be a much more peaceful place.

Here goes nothing. And everything.

We talk DJ.

"What music should play when the band breaks?" ("A smidge harder than light rock.")

"How long of a break should the DJ take?" ("Half an hour.")

"Did we pay her yet?" ("As we speak.")

We talk videographer.

"Where are all our baby pictures for the montage?" ("Shoebox under the bed.")

"How many hours of footage should they shoot?" ("Four. Extra for the director's cut.")

"VHS or DVD?" ("That's an easy one. Pure digital, baby.")

"Who will tape the preparties?" ("Drew. Yes, he'll try not to focus on breasts this time.")

"Did you send in the proposal tape for them to include?" ("Yup." My tongue still tastes like stamp.)

"Did we pay her yet?" ("As we speak.")

We talk photographer.

"When should we take family shots? Right after ceremony or a bit later?" ("Right after.")

"How many albums do we need?" ("Twenty? I don't know. Your call.")

"Where will they stand?" ("They're pros. They'll know where to stand.")

"Did we pay her yet?" ("As we speak.")

We talk food.

"Is a buffet classy enough?" ("Of course." Although I shouldn't have burped just then.)

"Do we have enough appetizers?" ("Plenty. About those pigs in blankets? No, you're right.")

"What should we feed the band? Buffet plate or something else?" ("What's cheaper, er, better?")

"Did we pay them yet?" ("As we speak.")

We talk drinks.

"Should we pay by the drink or by the hour?" ("Hour.")

"Top shelf or jug wine?" ("Anything in between?")

"How many cases of champagne?" ("One? Two? A dozen?")

"How many bartenders?" ("Two. No waiting.")

"Did we pay them yet?" ("As we speak.")

We talk limos.

"How will eighty guests go thirty miles in forty minutes?" ("No SAT math this early.")

"How do we get them back?" ("See previous answer.")

"Is there an early bus or do they stay until the end?" ("Let them suffer, er, enjoy it all.")

"Did we pay them yet?" ("As we speak.")

We talk infrastructure.

"Should we upgrade the chairs?" ("If you want.")

"Should we get more rain insurance?" ("If you want.")

"Should we rent heat lamps?" ("If you want.")

"Did we pay the coordinator yet?" ("As we speak.")

We talk talk.

"What will you say?" ("Don't worry. Really, don't worry. Seriously, don't worry.")

"When will people toast at the rehearsal dinner? Early or late?" ("Three cocktails early.")

"Did you send the readings to Brent and Ally?" ("As we speak.")

No money to shell out over this one. Woo-hoo.

Three hours later, right or wrong, cheaply or costly, we decide it all. Ending months of me not chiming in, chirping about, nor coughing up a comment. I need a shower.

✧

BUT THERE'S NO time to cleanse. This morning's discussion was a breeze compared to what I am about to face. My biggest fear. No, not telling my family we're having a church wedding.

My biggest wedding fear is dancing. I surprisingly impressed Deb by suggesting we take a few dance lessons. And I really blew her mind when I actually booked class time. Who knew there are crash courses in how to dance at your own wedding? Not me, especially since the last time I stepped foot into a dance studio was for break dancing lessons when I was fifteen. What a beating I got that week. My parachute pants were ripped to shreds. The cardboard box I used to bust a move was torched. My gold-plated chain was pawned. And that's just what I did to myself.

I convinced Karen, an almost-married coworker, to enroll with me. Strength in numbers. Plus, I had a feeling Karen's husband-to-be might be in the same position that I am in: barely adept at walking a straight line without bumping into something. Deb, on the other hand, took tap, jazz, and even hula lessons growing up. I doubt any of those steps will come up at our wedding, but at least she knows how to maneuver both her upper and lower body at the same time.

"It'll be okay, Craig. You can dance. You're a good dancer," Deb sympathizes.

"Correction," I say. "I am a good drunk dancer. I am not a good dancer."

"So you'll have a few drinks before the wedding. You don't think I'm going in sober?"

"You're talking a glass of champagne. I'm talking ten vodka tonics."

"If you must, you must. Just don't call me that old Oreos-loving girlfriend's name."

"That was once. Won't you ever forgive? At least forget?"

"Produce a girl baby and we'll see."

"Can we give her my old girlfriend's name?"

"Now you have to produce two baby girls."

"You know we have to have sex first."

"Three girls!"

✧

THERE ARE NINE other couples at the dance studio. I feel vindicated. I'm not the only schmuck with two left feet. We introduce ourselves. Most have months before their big day, and this is just the first step in a multi-tiered dance plan. For me, this was it. Do or die. I did spring for the Deluxe Package, which includes one more group session and two private lessons. So if I didn't *do* today, I'll at least have a few more chances before I *die*.

The music starts. A slow waltz. I assume my normal dancing position: finger-snapping, lip-biting, hip-swaying, feet locking like cement to the floor. A move guaranteed to compel any Good Samaritan to tackle me and shove straws in my mouth to prevent any tongue swallowing from the painful, twisted convulsions he or she just witnessed.

The other couples closely hold each other. Deb smirks. I grab. We're good to go. We learn a basic box step. It's not that bad. Heck, I'm not that bad. We take it up a notch. All the steps have follow a basic rhythm: slow, slow, quick, quick. The guy's part is easy compared to the girl's role. We move forward; they move backward. We stand around; they twirl around. We grab their ass; they wring our necks. And yet, even with all of these advantages, I feel my leadership taking a backseat. Deb's dancing experience begins to subvert any control I struggle to take.

To recover a semblance of manhood, I violently spin Deb across the room. A real move? Probably not. If this were actually our wedding, Deb would be face-first in the buffet table. Today all that happens is that I throw Deb into the arms of another man. One who seems to know how to dance. But I get some applause anyway. Okay, Deb gets the applause for staying upright through this ordeal, but we're a team, so I take credit with a simple bow.

What a team.

AND YOU THOUGHT PICKING MUSIC WAS TOUGH

AFFLICTED WITH TWO left feet?
Need to be drunk before stepping out?
Uncontrollably bite your lower lip whenever you dance?
Oh boy.

Your primary objective: Survive the first dance.

The dancing doesn't start until you hit center stage. You can slide right into these dances once you're introduced. Or save it until after you eat (but remember, no one should dance before you). Typically, this is the sequence of pairings that kick off the ceremony:

- ❥ Bride/groom. All eyes on you.
- ❥ Bride/Father and Groom/Mother. Be sure to return to your bride after this dance.
- ❥ Wedding party. Bride/groom and parents can continue to dance.
- ❥ All guests. If people are reluctant, have wedding party dance with them.

Dancing lesson: It's a good thing.

Most every dance studio (and yes, there are probably a dozen near where you live—go figure) offers wedding packages to get you ready for your first dance and keep you from embarrassing yourself the rest of the night. When you take the lessons, remember you won't be dancing at your wedding in jeans and high-tops. Think about what you'll be wearing. Think about what she'll be wearing. There's going to be a lot of uncomfortable clothes and shoes between the two of you.

Try to start a few months prior to the wedding to let the moves sink in. Plus, to give your fiancée's toes time to heal.

First dance choices

You have a lot of moves to pick from. Depending on your skill (and risk) level, think about doing one of the following steps: slow, waltz, foxtrot, rumba, hustle, salsa, swing, cha-cha, tango, two-step, west coast swing.

Did you scratch your head when you read this list? Take a lesson. Buy a video. Elope.

■

20 QUESTIONS WITH YOUR WEDDING VENDORS. MORE LIKE 20,000 QUESTIONS.

YOU'RE GOING TO meet a ton of wedding vendors. And pay a ton of money to get out in one piece. Here are a few questions you should ask. To impress the vendor. To impress your bride. Or to get out of the next visit.

And when you ask these questions, don't forget to lean in a bit when speaking. Intimidate where possible. Cave when necessary.

Wedding coordinator
- Do you work for a flat fee?
- Can we speak to some former clients?
- Do you attend each wedding?
- Do you come with us for each vendor meeting?
- How many weddings have you done?
- What types of packages do you offer?

Photographer
- Can we see pictures of your work?
- Can we contact former clients?
- How many photos do you plan on taking?
- Do you use digital cameras?
- Can we keep the negatives or digital copies?
- What style(s) will you employ (e.g., B&W, candid)?

Videographer

- Can we see videos of your work?
- Can we contact former clients?
- How long will you film?
- Do you use professional equipment?
- Is there a charge for additional tapes or DVDs?
- What type of lighting will you bring?
- How many cameras do you use?

Tuxedo store

- (If out-of-town wedding) Can we pick up tuxes at a local shop?
- Is the groom's tux free?
- Do you have other locations where groomsmen can be fitted?

Bridal dress store

- How long does it take to make/alter the dress?
- Can you store the dress until the wedding?
- How many fittings do you offer?
- Why am I talking to you blindfolded?

Florist

- Is there an extra charge for delivery, setup, or breakdown?
- How many events will you do this day?
- Can you preserve any flowers for keepsake?
- Have you worked at our location before?
- Do you have any references?

Officiant

- (If applicable) Is it okay we are from different religions?
- (If applicable) Is it okay if one/both of us are divorced?
- (If applicable) Do we have to belong to your church or synagogue?
- Can we write our own vows?
- Do we have to have counseling?

Ceremony location

- How many guests can we have?
- Can we take pictures inside?
- Can we videotape the ceremony?
- What music can we play?
- Are there any attire guidelines?

Reception location

- How many guests can we have?
- Are there other events planned the same day?
- Do you offer other services (e.g., catering)?
- Are we required to use certain services (e.g., linens)?
- Are there any usage (e.g., decoration, music, alcohol) restrictions?
- How many hours do we have the location for?

Caterer

- Is there a guaranteed minimum number of guests?
- Can we do a taste testing?
- How many servers will there be (there should be at least one server for every ten guests)?
- Can you make my mom's meatloaf?
- What is the cost per person for food? What about alcohol costs?

Cake baker

- What designs can you do?
- Can we do a taste testing?
- Is there a setup charge?

Music

- What is your song list?
- Do you have all the equipment you need?
- Do you have music samples?
- Can you do special requests?
- Can we see you in action?

Transportation

- What cars do you offer?
- Do you provide champagne or other drinks?
- Can we speak to former clients?
- Is there a cleaning fee?
- Do you offer a multi-car discount?

Stationery

- What types of printing process do you offer?
- What is your turnaround time?
- How many weddings do you do in a year?
- Can you produce all of the materials (announcement, invitation, response cards, thank-you notes, party favors, maps, place cards, wedding program)?
- Do you offer calligraphy services?

Honeymoon planner

- What travel requirements are there (e.g., visa, vaccinations)?
- Do you offer travel insurance?
- Do you have a twenty-four-hour contact number?
- What are the local customs of our travel destinations?

3

WHEN THE PLANNING GETS TOUGH, I'M ALREADY GONE.

Two weeks to go

New to-do's

Pick up license

Time to head to the clerk's office and sign your life away. Go
as a couple and bring proper identification (document needs
to have both your picture and signature). If this isn't your
first marriage, be prepared to say when your last one ended. If
it's recent, you may need to show a certified copy of the
divorce or death certificate.

It shouldn't take too long to complete this task. Do something fun afterward.

Remind groomsmen of rehearsal and wedding details

Besides telling your friends to take it easy on the still-single
women guests, you should take the time to explain any special
seating requirements or other wedding details. In addition, give
the officiant's fee to best man. Preferably in check form. Especially if groomsmen are prone to hanging out at strip joints.

Old to-do's left to do

	How late am I?
Shop for honeymoon clothes	2 months
Help fiancée with Couple's Shower thank-you notes	2 months
Pick up wedding rings	2 months
Pour your heart out (write vows, speeches, and toast)	1 week
Verify honeymoon reservation	1 week

UP THE CREEK
WITH TOO MANY PADDLES.

Never go to bed mad. Stay up and fight.
(Phyllis Diller)

FOR ONCE, I am supposed to wake up early. We're going on a white-water rafting trip—Deb figured we could benefit from a break in wedding planning. A chance to get away. A chance to rediscover ourselves. And seeing how things have progressed, maybe a chance to talk like a happy couple again. The timing couldn't have been more perfect. All that is missing is a time machine to roll back an entire year of missed conversations, intimate moments, and dinners together without mention of budgets, guests, or flowers. But alas, no time machine. Just an apartment full of brand-new rafting gear: dry sacks, helmets, life jackets, oars, and three waterproof cameras (for posterity's sake).

"We will be doing this all the time," Deb said as we purchased seven hundred dollars' worth of gear at REI. Gear we both knew would probably end up lost in our garage. Once we can afford a garage.

I am not sure I believed Deb, but as long as the purchase

didn't involve lace, engravings, or fancy foods, I considered it money well spent.

We grab armfuls of stuff and head for the car.

"Keys?" I ask.

"Great," she replies.

We hobble down the stairs and reach the car. I stare. She stares. I speak.

"How could you not have the keys?"

"You said you had the keys."

"I asked if you had the keys."

"You said."

"I asked."

"It's cold."

"At least you have the house keys."

Now it's my turn to stare.

"You're kidding? What are we going to do?"

"Maybe I can break into the apartment?"

But like any protective fiancé, I jammed wood in our window frames to prevent break-ins. Have I provided too well for the household?

"We need to leave." Deb's annoyed.

"You need to relax." I'm scrambling.

"You need to shut up."

The apartment manager lives on our floor, but we're not sure where. No sense of playing rock, scissors, paper to decide who gets to be the weirdo knocking on doors. After waking six neighbors, I finally locate the manager and save the day.

✦

SO WE'RE FORTY-FIVE minutes late. Deb isn't talking to me. No big deal. There's still plenty of time to be a carefree couple again. I'll just step on the gas and make up time on the road.

"Laugh it off. A slight speed bump in our day," I chuckle.

"You mean speed trap. Cop." Now she laughs.

I'm now two hundred dollars poorer, and my license is one point richer. Deb is still laughing at me. It's still early. I'll make it up on the water.

134

By the time we arrive, the morning's antics have burnt off. The river is roaring, the air is fresh, the sun is out and our day officially begins. As captain of our ship, I command my first and only mate to launch our two-man raft into the water.

"We don't need keys for this do we, oh Captain?" Deb asks.

I smell mutiny. "No need, you landlubber. Now heave-ho before I make ye walk the plank," I bellow from the back of the raft.

Unfortunately, the river has a mind of its own. We try to steer with all our might, but something's not working. Maybe because I'm paddling and Deb's just watching the trees go by. Which is quite challenging, as we are stuck in a perpetual three-hundred-and-sixty-degree spiral.

"Paddle right," I scream.

"Paddle left?" I ask.

"Paddle please," I beg.

Finally, Deb paddles. But her excellent timing on the dance floor doesn't carry over to the river. It would almost be better if we were at total odds against each other. Then we'd only be standing still. However, when I hard left, she soft rights. When I soft right, she hard lefts. When I start, she stops. And yes, when I stop, she starts. All in all, we manage to sink our unsinkable raft eight times. Should the fact that we are not in sync as a couple be troubling? Are the rhythms (well, mis-rhythms) of our paddling signifying something about the rhythms of life? Should Dr. Phil be paddling up besides us with one of his life lessons? Or interventions?

✧

WE'RE SOAKING WET. The other rafters, guides, and a few chipmunks are laughing. There's still half a river to complete.

"Our guide said the key to a successful voyage is listening to the man in back. The MAN in back," I offer.

"The guide's an idiot and so are you," Deb responds. "I take that back. That would be insulting to idiots."

After our ninth capsizing, Deb insists on taking the helm. For about a minute I follow her lead. We move. Forward. Efficiently. But that's not fair. I am good at helping her. Why isn't she good at helping me? Spite takes over. Must I always follow? How can I regain the lead? Am I not leading because I'm not asking for the right help?

Too much introspection. Capsize number ten.

I try to salvage the day. "At least we're not talking about the wedding."

✧

WE DON'T TALK about the wedding on the drive back. In fact, we don't speak the whole drive back. The day is almost over, but there's always time at home to save the day.

I unload the car. Deb's waiting on the couch and unloads on me.

"Are you sure you want to get married?" she asks.

"Why are you asking this?"

"I just want to know your heart's into this. Into me."

"Yes."

"Because if you have something to say to me, you better say it now. Not a year from now. Or ten years. Or fifty."

"Fifty? Come on. At that point, I think even I will not have any doubts that we're truly stuck with each other."

"Seriously, this day really sucked. Is this what I'm in for?" She has a point.

"We don't live on a houseboat, so I'm not too worried about more capsizing. I think we can stay dry most of the time."

"Forget capsizing, what about communicating?"

"I think we're communicating. You might not like what we're communicating, but we're communicating. Give or take our hours of silence."

"There's nothing you're hiding from me?"

Uh-oh. Now that's a loaded question. "What would I be hiding from you?"

"How you feel about marrying. Marrying me."

"I'm the neurotic one. I worry about you marrying me. Not the other way around."

"Maybe you don't worry about marrying me, but someone does."

Now I'm half-exasperated, half-wondering if she has planted probes in my brain. "What are you talking about?"

"There's no one who's been talking marriage with you?"

"If you think someone's been talking marriage with me, I'd be doing such a crummy job planning?" Any time is a good time to admit your weaknesses. Some women find this endearing.

"Not about the planning of. About the doing it." Endearing. Endangering. It's all good, right?

"No one's been talking nothing with me."

"What about this?" Deb pulls out an envelope Cousin Isaac sent me a few months ago. A envelope meant for my eyes only. And now it's an envelope that Deb was holding onto for the right moment. No more using the computer cable box for any personal stash.

I squint, trying to make it seem that I don't have a clue what Deb's talking about. But I do. "It doesn't mean anything." No time to be pissed that she was snooping. Although that is a big thing. I don't want a wife that I can't trust to let me have some secrets.

"It means people would rather you still look for that nice Jewish girl. Which isn't me."

"It's just some newspaper articles. Silly stuff."

"You mean you read, no, even glanced at this one and didn't get that point," Deb questions as she jams *Staying Jewish* in my face.

"Like I said, that doesn't mean anything." I have to do better than that. My eyes scan the room for salvation. Or maybe I should focus really hard on the paper and set it on fire like Superman?

"What about this?" Deb shoves *How to Be a Jew* into my chest.

Did these articles actually mean something to me? Was I trying to get caught? Did I want this conversation to come out? Have I not resolved my own feelings about religion? Or did I just want Deb to think I have doubts and be forced to love me more?

Deb continues. "Do you not want to be with me? Do you want to find a Jewish girl? Do you even love me?"

"Of course." Vagueness doesn't seem to be the right approach. "Of course I want to be with you. Of course I don't want to leave you for a Jewish girl. Of course I love you. But what about this?" I grab the latest issue of *Catholic Family* from the coffee table (I guess Catholics are better at showcasing their guilt) and throw it at Deb. She has a lifetime subscription. A gift from Deb's old parish. The one that keeps calling wondering when we're going to drop by.

But the bedroom door slams before she sees it. I slip it under the door, opened to page twelve, *He Might Be Confused, but Don't Confuse the Kids.*

This isn't a new argument. We have talked about religion before, but only up to a point. Should I be worried about what happens with our kids? Will Deb become more religious once we have children? Will she insist on Catholic school? Will I become more religious? Will I stop eating pork chops? Deb said she'll support both traditions, but not on her own. I need to step up. Is now the right time? I'm not just going to wake up religious one day. But I also don't want to lose my heritage. Does honoring my heritage mean attending temple every week? Or just being a good person?

Another night to be glad we have Deb's comfortable couch. Too bad I'll never get custody of it.

ALREADY COUNTED TO 10?
BLOOD PRESSURE UP TO 500?
1,000 TO-DO'S LEFT?

TAKE A TIME-OUT and try one of these stress relief suggestions.

Worst case: you'll have fun.

Best case: your fiancée might have fun, too.

- Go for a run.
- Hit the gym.
- Walk the dog.
- Get a dog. Then walk the dog.
- Write a letter.
- Write a book (boy, you are really stressed).
- Have sex (typically with fiancée).
- Play basketball, paintball, or golf.
- See a movie.
- Get drunk.
- Go out for dinner.
- Get a massage.
- Go away for weekend.
- Buy an Xbox. Or visit someone who has one.
- Go to a ballgame.
- Apply to a reality TV show.
- Build or destroy something.
- Go to Las Vegas or at least a Chuck E. Cheese.
- Google ex-girlfriends.
- Watch SportsCenter (again).

ROSES ARE RED.
VIOLETS ARE BLUE.
I THINK I'M DEAD.
BASED ON JUST ONE LITTLE CLUE.

Marriage is grand.
Divorce is ten grand!
(Rev. Dr. Adamovich)

"HELLO? DEB?"

The apartment is empty. There's not even a note by the key rack (nor are there keys). This hasn't happened before, but there are many things that haven't happened before. Deb's cell phone is on the coffee table. Not unusual. So there's nothing to worry about, right? Where is she?

✧

THE PHONE RINGS. Time for me to apologize.

I kneel. She'll sense this. "Deb?"

"No. May I speak to Deb?"

I rise. "She's not here, and we don't want what you're selling. Please take us off your call list." For once, I'll be tough with a telemarketer.

"Is this Craig?"

"Yes. Who is this?"

"I'm Chris, your florist."

I have a florist?

"I wanted to say that I am sorry about the change in plans."

Deb changes things all the time. No big deal, I reassure myself.

"And that since we are so close to the wedding date, we'll only be able to return half of your payment for those flowers."

I am on the floor again. Not kneeling, but laying face down. "Who are you again?"

"The florist."

"Of course. Thanks for letting us know. Have a good day."

Did Deb cancel our wedding? Because of yesterday? Did I really fuck things up? It wasn't that bad. She couldn't. She wouldn't. She hasn't done this before. Is this a cry for attention? Because tears are forming. How could one argument yester day (okay, four arguments) cause her to call off the wedding? Maybe it's not just yesterday, but all days. All those missed opportunities to shine.

Tears are releasing. Breathing is heavier. One hand on heart. Other on head. My world is crashing down. Life without Deb is like life without life. I can't believe she called off the wedding.

✧

WHO DO I call?

My mom? Too early. I need confirmation before I open that conversation up. She'll be on a plane trying to save the day before I can finish my first sob-filled sentence.

Deb's mom? Too uncomfortable. What would I say? "Hi. It's Craig. You know, your future-ex-son-in-law. Or is it ex-future-son-in-law? Anyway, have you seen Deb? She canceled the wedding and—what do you know—forgot to tell me? If you do see her, please have her call. By the way do you know when it's an acceptable time to report the engagement ring stolen and start dating again?"

Patrick.

"You can't really blame her, can you?" Patrick offers.

Now I'm totally freaking out. Is Patrick more perceptive than me? Why hasn't he said anything before? Would I have the balls to say something like this to my friend?

"Whose side are you on? What should I do?"

"Go to work?" Typical guy response. "Act like it never happened."

"But something has happened. What would you do?"

"Go to a strip joint?" Why can't guys stop joking and really talk? Is this my fate as a joker? Is this my fate as a man?

"Come on. There's no need for Deb to find my car in Chinatown parked under a neon 'Always Open' sign."

"You could take a cab."

✧

THE PHONE RINGS again. I try again. "Deb?"

"Deb? No, it's Mom."

Does Mom have ESP and could sense her son's in trouble across three time zones?

"I'm still not sure what dress to wear," Mom says. Her attire has been a long-standing debate. One that I can't help at all. For all practical (read: stylistic) purposes, I'm color-blind. Who knew blue socks and brown shoes didn't go together. And three sets of stripes really don't mesh well. Reason number eighty-seven to appreciate Deb.

"Either one will been fine."

"Brown or tan?"

Like I know the difference. "You'll look beautiful in anything you wear."

"Such a nice son. Such a good catch. Deb's lucky."

"I know." Well I don't know about Deb being lucky. I know that I'm lucky. Well, I hope that I'm still lucky.

✧

FORTUNATELY I HAVE not spilled the beans to either mom yet. There has to be something I can do to salvage this. Think, Craig. Think. Isn't there anything my MBA taught me? This is just like any other negotiation. Deb and I just haven't found mutually agreeable terms yet. The only difference is that while I think there's still positive interdependence to be had (namely, our engagement is a cooperative, both-sides-win situation), Deb has realized that the key to being a strong negotiator is the ability to walk away from the table (namely, I'm screwed).

Did Deb really leave me? Is this it? I thought a breakup of this magnitude would have been more dramatic. Plates breaking. Name calling. Police intervention. The things you see in movies or read about in books. Eventful moments. Moments that make people think "My God, what have I done? Have I thrown away all the good for just one bad?" Even if that one bad is me? I'm not that bad. Am I? And this isn't very eventful. Or is it? It's just me sitting and wondering. And yes, still crying.

Should I roam the streets looking for Deb and beg for forgiveness? That's a movie moment. Cut to strong, silent (and handsome) lead actor driving eighty in a school zone, crashing car into the front of a hospital and grabbing the ready-to-forgive (and beautiful) lead actress and kissing her though the end credits.

Okay, maybe I won't speed by schoolchildren and destroy private property. More like I'll go to our favorite local hangout, see Deb sobbing at our corner table, slide right in, and scoop her away and tell her everything will be okay.

Or is this my opportunity to reclaim all of my freedom? Forget marriage, I just got the ultimate hall pass. Should I find a new favorite hangout; see a pretty woman also sobbing at a corner table because she, too, just broke up with someone; slide right in; and become her rebound guy? Rebound sex would be good. It's amazing how quickly one's mind wanders. Would Deb think about rebound sex at this point? Of course, Deb's rebound sex would be with that Catholic guy from the bar with a fancy car and huge savings account (yes, I now made him Catholic).

Would it take Deb a few days or months to recover from me? Maybe years? I'm not worth waiting years.

No! I will fight for Deb. She's not getting out of this so easily.

And "fight" for me entails sitting on the couch (TV off) thinking, "Come back, Deb. Come back."

Two hours later, Deb does come back. As if nothing's wrong.

"How could you do this to me?" I ask, back on my knees.

"Oh, sorry I forgot to leave a note. Don't be so dramatic," Deb responds.

"Like it would be better if you wrote 'wedding's off'?"

"What are you talking about?"

"Our florist called. His condolences meant a lot to me."

"What?"

"He told me our wedding is canceled."

"That's not true."

"You didn't cancel it?"

"No."

"Did your mom?" I ask.

"Did *your* mom?" Deb retorts.

I didn't think of that one. "No. What about the roses? No roses equal no wedding."

"All I did was switch to lilies. They'll look better on the tables," Deb explains.

"Oh."

"Oh? You need help."

"What would you think?"

"Not that. Why must you hold on to a fight longer than necessary? We fought. You're wrong. Fight over. You're not winning me over to your faith by acting this way. It's not all about life and death struggles."

"Oh yeah, well where were you then?"

"Thought you might like something fun for dinner tonight." Deb holds up a Safeway bag and pulls out a brightly-colored box. With dinosaurs on it.

Macaroni and cheese. My favorite. I melt.

"Sorry about yesterday."

"What? Like that was our first fight. Why aren't you at work?"

"I needed to see you." And learn more about your strange ways. I'm glad I'll never experience any rebound sex. Deb and I do take part in a good makeup sex session, and that is fine by me. Especially midday, not-going-to-work makeup sex.

BRIDES FOR SALE. BRIDES FOR SALE. BRIDES FOR SALE.

IN ANCIENT TIMES, husbands could buy as many brides as he could afford. Wives were often prisoners in their own houses. Many married women ranked just above cattle in terms of standing in their community. And to add insult to injury, dowries became the property of their husbands, who might sell it for cash.

Today, approximately three out of five American wives are employed at least part-time. But that's only part of their financial worth. If the average American wife and mother were paid for the counseling, chauffeuring, cooking, household management, and other services she provides, it would total over $725,000 per year. That could buy a lot of manservants. Or at least should make their husbands be a little more appreciative. Hint, hint.

Source: Ric Edelman, author of *The Truth about Money* (ricedelman.com)

■

DON'T CROSS THAT LINE. DON'T EVEN GET CLOSE.

THERE MIGHT BE a great deal of things you can get away with normally, but wedding planning is not a normal time. To avoid having to return the gifts, move out of state, and change your identity, here's a list of things NOT to do to your fiancée.

- Cancel fiancée's credit cards (especially if they're not in your name)—no matter how much she is spending on flowers.
- Casually date—no matter how tempting it looks.

- Demand only AC/DC songs at wedding—no matter how many posters of Angus and Malcolm Young you had growing up.
- Stare longer than one second at anyone else—no matter if looking away would instantly blind you by the sun.
- Have more than one bachelor party—no matter how many friends missed the first one.
- Book alone time for yourself during the honeymoon—no matter how many PGA tournaments were held at the resort.
- Criticize *any* part of the wedding plans—no matter how much or little you have helped.

yours

mine

WHAT'S MINE IS YOURS, AND WHAT'S YOURS IS YOURS.

When a girl marries,
she exchanges the attention of many men
for the inattention of one.
(Helen Rosland)

IT MIGHT BE the afterglow of post-makeup sex (and post-post-makeup sex), but I want to be different. Different for Deb. Different for me. The argument wasn't necessary. Deb didn't need to be upset. Why fight the wedding and the happily every after? I can't remember how many times have I thought this, but at this point, we're T minus two weeks. Maybe I should stop and smell the roses (or is it now lilies?). Especially at the rates Chris the florist is charging us.

Why can't I let go of my worries and embrace what's about to happen? I don't plan on stopping the wedding. And now I know Deb's not going to, either. Maybe the wedding will be fun after all?

Maybe Deb will be interested in some post-epiphany sex?

No such luck.

TIME TO THINK like the responsible head of household I am about to become. Responsible people follow through on their responsible promises, and today I should follow through on a financial promise. Opening our first joint bank account. Deb meets me at the bank to sign the papers.

"Just to recap, it's not really a joint account. We won't be jointly depositing and jointly withdrawing. I deposit. You withdraw. Right?" I ask Deb.

"For now. Once I finish nursing school, it'll be time for you to take a work break," Deb sweetly replies.

"How am I supposed to take time off when you're pregnant and taking care of the kids?"

"Who said I'm doing that? You *have* expressed a desire to be Mr. Mom."

"Only if Mrs. Dad makes enough to replenish our joint account."

"You worry too much."

"And you spend too much."

"Folks, folks. How about we get back to picking a check design?" Mike, our personal banker pleads.

"Plain," I offer. They can't charge more for plain, can they?

"Flowers," Deb counters. "Roses. No, lilies. No, roses. Lilies." Way to up the ante.

"Lilies, it is," Mike states. Way to pick sides.

I am merely delaying the inevitable by not combining all of our monies now. I know we agreed to keep most things separate, but what's the point? Do I want to have a secret stash, just in case? Are we going to be a couple who hides its purchases?

Would Deb care if I bought a new gadget? Would I care if she bought a . . . what does Deb really buy for herself? I don't know. Should I? Does she already have a secret stash of stuff? Where's her computer cable box, full of hidden jewelry and other expensive items? Is there anything for me? I actually hope not. I love the fact that Deb buys me things, but I'm pretty picky about my toys. Hopefully after we're married, I can simply hand her a list of part numbers to buy and act surprised when I open the presents. Yes, it eliminates most of the fun. Like me fighting over the definition of "joint account." But that's part of my charm.

As Deb steps away to take a call, Mike leans in to me.

"Are you sure you know what you're doing?" Mike whispers.

I lean back. "I wouldn't be here if I didn't know what I was doing." Arms crossed. Head nodding, full of confidence. Previous mental anguish notwithstanding.

"You are aware that either one of you will be able to clean out your joint account."

I lean in. "How many times does that happen?" Arms open. Head shaking, full of fear. Previous mental anguish now standing front and center.

"Enough for me to warn you. You know, guy to guy."

"Any tips?"

"Don't screw around."

"Haven't heard that one yet. Thanks."

No need to worry. First of all, our account balance will probably be stuck in triple digits for at least a few years. Second, I know Deb wouldn't do that. Or would she? I shoot a loving smile toward Deb as she reads a poster on home mortgages. Smile back and I'll sign the papers.

Come on Deb, smile. Turn around. Look into my eyes and smile your love back to me. At least see the terror-induced tremor in my lips and shoot me an "I've got you by the balls" smile. That'll do, too.

Teeth. Friendly, white teeth. Phew.

To celebrate our jointness, we pay for lunch from our new account. And considering how low our opening balance is, I imagine an alarm going off on Mike's computer that causes him to think, "Damn, she's quick."

✧

BACK AT WORK, I add Deb to my stock portfolio, life insurance, medical plan, 401(k), AAA card, and Costco membership. I draw the line on keeping my AOL Instant Messenger screen name, but that's about it. The wedding web (and not the craiganddeb.com one) wraps tighter and tighter around me. With each signature, any escape gets more and more complex. But that's assuming I care about keeping a free annual prostate exam and two car tows per year all to myself. What the heck. What's mine is hers, right?

After all, living together with Deb for the past year allows me to already know Deb's pros (she's an awesome cook) and cons (she's an awful cleaner). And she knows mine, especially my snoring, sneaker piling, and need to plug at least twenty things into each power outlet. I believe it's important to learn as much about each other before taking the plunge. Always make an informed decision. Even if that reduces the new couple smell. I wouldn't want to cross into husbandhood not knowing that my wife talks to an ex-boyfriend at least once a day. I'd rather find this out while in fiancéland and have time to kick the ex's ass (or at least block his number from her phones).

OUR FIRST PRIVATE dance lesson is tonight. Considering my previous stellar performance in group, Serge, our instructor, fast-forwards to the advanced steps. Does he think I have talent? Boy, do I fool him.

"SLOOOOW. SLOOOOW. QUICK. QUICK," Serge implores.

I reply with a quick, slow, slow, quick. "It'll come back to me. Trust me."

"SLOOOOW. SLOOOOW. QUICK. QUICK."

It's not happening. Deb is steaming. I am sweating. Serge is screaming. Too many steps. Too much work. Go here. Now there. Hands up. Knees bent. Smile. The beats. The moves. The coordination. The humiliation.

I cut the lesson short. "We'll practice at home. Promise."

I'm wiped for the day. I even mess up the plop on the couch and land my ass on the floor. But in knocking off a cushion, I find a five-dollar bill under the love seat. All isn't lost. That money should be enough to pay for one dry roll at the wedding dinner. Butter, of course, will cost extra.

WHAT'S MINE IS MINE!
PRENUPTIAL AGREEMENTS.

A PRENUPTIAL AGREEMENT expresses how a couple will divide property, obtain inheritances, define spousal support, and carve up businesses when their marriage ends. Not a nice conversation, but could be important if your last name is Getty, Rockefeller, or Hilton.

Couples sometimes include personal preferences into the prenups as well. You specify things like who will do the dishes, the frequency of sexual activities expected, and how your children will be educated. As long as you don't specify anything illegal or contrary to public policy, feel free to include whatever you want. Keep in mind, however, these preferences may be hard to enforce, let alone be agreed to in the first place. Good luck!

Just be sure the agreement is in writing and drafted with a lawyer or a well-written template. In most states, oral prenuptial agreements are not valid. Even if you tape-record her saying "blow jobs until I die," you won't have a chance in court.

■

THE MONEY SHOT

SORRY, NOT THE fun kind.

Soon, you'll be sharing the same bed and PIN. It's better to talk money before the wedding. Last thing you want to find out is that she has more money troubles than Enron. Or can't resist investing in timeshares.

First, do the math. Calculate how much each of you has in:

- ❧ Income: salary, investments, and dividends.
- ❧ Expenses: household and fun.
- ❧ Savings: bank accounts, stocks, 401(k), and IRAs.
- ❧ Assets: house, jewelry, stamp collections, etc.

- Long-term debt: mortgages and student loans.
- Short-term debt: credit cards, bookies, etc.

Second, talk turkey:

- Should you have individual accounts, one joint account or both?
- How much money do you require to feel financially secure?
- How much money should you save each month and where should it be put?
- What types of purchases require joint agreement?
- Who will pay the bills?
- How much insurance should each of you have?
- How do you want to save/invest for the long term?

Finally, sign your life away. Remember to add your fiancée on your accounts and change your beneficiaries. Some accounts to review include:

- Insurance: homeowner/rental, auto, life, medical, dental, and disability.
- Financial: credit cards and bank, investment, and retirement accounts.
- Assets: home title and car registration.
- Utilities: phone, gas/electric, garbage, cable/satellite, water, etc.

And don't forget about death (do you have a will already?) and taxes (you have a new filing status coming up).

BIG SCREEN
DREAMS.

> I feel sure that no girl could go to the altar,
> and would probably refuse, if she knew all.
> (Queen Victoria)

"WINE GLASSES. THAT'S ... great," I say.

The endless barrage of breakable presents is getting to me. We can't fit more than five people into our apartment without being forced into a game of Twister, but we're well on our way to host formal dinners for twelve. To no one in particular, I beg for a reprieve. "Puh-lease."

Of course, Deb answers my call. "When else will people buy these things for us?"

"What about something for me?"

"Last I checked, you like to eat. And drink."

"I know, but ..."

"Would any gift make you happy?"

I stand at a crossroads. Should I seize the moment, reveal Patrick's TV plot, and try to rally Deb for support? Or should I keep my mouth shut, open another soup bowl, and let sleeping dogs lie?

"Well . . . you see Patrick . . ." I watch her eyes. They blink. Good sign. " . . . is getting some people together for a wedding gift."

"For you?"

"For us. It's a little on the informal side, but we'll use it a lot. Guaranteed."

Deb's eyes widen. An eternity passes before she blinks. "Spill it."

"A big-screen TV."

"No."

"Yes. We can cuddle on the couch. I'll let you drive the remote . . . within reason, of course."

"A big screen? You're diverting our precious gift dollars away from our place settings?"

"Not me. Patrick. I just found out."

"Liar!"

Another eternity passes. Then something wonderful happens. "Well, just what TV are we getting?" Deb sighs.

"Up to us. In fact, I'll even let you pick."

"Well . . ."

That's good enough for me. I scoop Deb off the couch, pull her into the biggest hug imaginable, and spin her just as Serge taught me. I mentally apologize to the downstairs neighbors who are scurrying around their apartment searching for the safety of archways and bathtubs, convinced that a 7.8 quake is about to split San Francisco open.

WE RACE TOWARD Circuit City, stopping only to get coffee for my lovely, understanding, compassionate, and beautiful bride.

"Enough, Craig. I already agreed. Put some of this energy to good use for once."

I'm golden. Circuit City doesn't sell china and its gift certificates are nonrefundable. Whether Deb likes it or not, I'm getting a big-screen TV. *The Blues Brothers* as it's supposed to be seen: in eye-ruining glory. And heard. Because once we get the TV, the next step is buying the five-hundred-watts-per-channel Dolby digital surround sound system. Just like what we've done with home furnishings ("But we need new curtains to go with the rug.

And of course the tables won't match, so we'll need to replace them as well. Plus . . .").

We are surrounded by scores of TVs. My confidence strengthens, ready for battle. I am prepared. I know my resources. I know my enemy. I know my strategy. We can neither afford nor fit a monster-sized TV in our place, so I have opted for just a healthy dose of gigantism. I stand in front of a modest forty-inch Sony that I have been researching during my off hours. Six separate inputs, high-definition ready, enhanced cinema widescreen, dual-tuner picture-in-picture. Forty-six-function remote control.

Deb walks right past me and my sensible pick and parks herself in front of a TV with its own ZIP code.

"Is this what we're getting?" she asks.

"I was thinking about something more reasonable."

"Why be reasonable? This one is huge. Live a bit."

"But I don't think we'll get enough money for this one. Now the one over here fits perfectly."

"And why can't we pay for the difference?"

I can't really argue that logic. More like I shouldn't. But, of course, I do. "We can't afford it."

"You're kidding. You want a big-screen TV. I'm letting you get an even bigger big screen. And . . ."

She is right. What am I doing? "But, what about saving for other stuff? Like braces for our kids?"

"Let me get this straight. We're not married yet. And with your utter lack of helping, I am still not sure you really want to get married. We don't have kids. We're not going to have kids for a while. But you're worried about spending a few hundred more on a TV today because we won't be able to get braces for these imaginary kids from our imaginary wedding?"

"Deb, have you seen pictures of my teeth, pre-railroad tracks?"

"What's wrong with you?"

"I don't know a good thing when I see it?"

"And . . ."

"I should keep my neuroses to myself?"

"And . . ."

"We're not getting a big-screen TV?"

We leave that wonderful store of stores in silence. So much for Deb rallying more troops for gift certificates.

WE ARE VERY late in picking photos for the videographer to incorporate into the wedding DVD. And we need a photo album to display at the wedding for guests to ooh and ahh over. Preferably during our first dance. After double-washing and disinfecting my pizza grease-ridden hands, I throw myself head first into a shoebox full of pictures from our parents' weddings, family vacations, and us as kids.

I have to admit, I was a cute kid. Deb was really cute, too, but she still is. I was white-blonde (compared with today's dirty brown) and wasn't afraid to show off my bottle or my tummy, which everyone used to rub and call a beer belly. The pictures of me double-fisting bottles stopped after I turned four, then resurfaced about seventeen years later. The same time coincidentally as my belly resurfaced. Or more appropriately, erupted.

I'm glad my parents saved enough for my braces. I guess I'll be able to afford lots of railroad tracks for my offspring with all that money that's not going to the big-screen TV.

NEED TO CALM HER NERVES?
HEAD TO THE VIDEO STORE.

SO IT WON'T be *Blade Runner*. Or even *Cannonball Run*. But if you come home with one of these movies and a bottle of wine, you'll be sure to lift her spirits.

Four Weddings and a Funeral

Runaway Bride
(just hide her Nike's)

The Philadelphia Story

The Wedding Singer

High Society

My Big Fat Greek Wedding

The Wedding Planner

Royal Wedding

Meet the Parents / Fockers

Seven Brides for Seven Brothers

American Wedding

The Wedding March

Saved by the Bell: Wedding in Las Vegas (no that wasn't my inspiration)

Father of the Bride (I and II)

My Best Friend's Wedding

It Happened One Night

Like Water for Chocolate

Green Card

Wedding Crashers

Monsoon Wedding

Muriel's Wedding

The Wedding Banquet

Honeymoon in Vegas

The In-Laws

A Wedding

And just in case you want to go off-list, please, please, please avoid these movies:

Sleeping with the Enemy

Suspicion

Gaslight

Rosemary's Baby

Dial M for Murder

(IN)DECISION-O-MATIC

DO YOU SUFFER from an utter lack of style, taste, and etiquette?

Are you faced with too many wedding decisions for one man to handle?

Whenever confronted with a wedding question, don't panic. Just answer her question with a question of your own that will be sure to get her thinking. Put the ball back in her court.

➤ Is that in our budget?
➤ What do you think?
➤ Why don't we split the difference?
➤ Would that be what your mom wants?
➤ Will it match your complexion?
➤ Isn't that a seasonal thing?
➤ How will that look to our guests?
➤ Do we have time to do that?
➤ Aren't the programs already printed?
➤ Did she really say we could do that?
➤ Does it go with our wedding theme?
➤ Didn't we already decide on that?
➤ Is it worth the trouble?
➤ Did you sleep on it?
➤ What does your horoscope say?
➤ What did your planning book say?
➤ What did the planner say?
➤ Did they do that at the last wedding we went to?
➤ Didn't you think about this one before?

THE HAIRCUT
HEARD ROUND THE CITY.

Keep your eyes wide open before marriage,
half shut afterwards.
(Benjamin Franklin)

MY LAST HAIRCUT as a free man. As I drive to my salon (yes, a salon, and no, not just because I'm about to get married), I think about how everything is about to switch from pre- to post-wedding status. An inescapable sense of finality hits me. I ponder the mundane to the spectacular. Will kisses be the same? Will holidays feel different? How about my paycheck? That one's easy—good-bye, slush funds. Hello, family savings account.

For most, a last haircut would fall pretty low on the "Gee, I wish it wouldn't end like this" list. But not me. My haircuts have always been more spiritual than physical. Sure, it's just an expensive bowl cut, but I am about to dramatically alter a relationship that's at least three times longer than the time I've been with Deb thus far. Brooke, my stylist, is happy for me, but is it all going to be different during my next rinse and cut? Brooke's been my cutter, confidante, and lover. Maybe not lover, but until now there's always been the chance.

Every three weeks we tell all. She's seen me at my best (meeting Deb; tongue-tied, star struck, and totally in love) and worst (waxing my back before a romantic trip with a previous girlfriend, looking like the poster child for a chicken pox vaccine). Brooke is a big supporter of Deb. Especially since Deb likes my haircuts.

"The usual?" Brooke coyly asks.

"Better make it a Super. Last one before the plunge."

"Let's hear it . . ."

Since meeting Brooke, I've moved to Chicago, back to California, to New York, and finally back to California, but we've held on. And even when I was a few thousand miles away, I'd plan trips back west just as I started to get shaggy up top. Of course, I have cheated on Brooke. But she always forgave me. Especially when I just had an affair with a twelve-dollar Supercuts special. Okay, I would usually get that cheap haircut just before heading back to California to make Brooke feel really missed.

Deb thinks my obsession with Brooke is odd, especially since I have never seen her outside the salon. But yet, she has been a big part of my life. I think it shows great devotion and commitment on my part, but concede there are probably some umbilical-cord-not-being-fully-trimmed issues beneath the surface. Of course, it doesn't hurt that she's gorgeous and never mentions her dating life. As if she's been waiting for me to step up to the plate all these years. But I couldn't risk a good haircut. Or could I?

"Perfection as usual," I tell Brooke. "See you in three."

"Bring the wife next time."

"We'll see." Like I want these worlds colliding. But why wouldn't I?

✧

I'M STILL NOT sure how I feel about getting my last haircut, so I attempt to seek comfort from others. Google to the rescue. "Groom wedding forum" returns a few interesting results. Apparently, we grooms are a chatty bunch. At least under the cloak of anonymity. I start a new discussion thread.

Topic: To help or not to help?
Author: SF_Groom2be

Hi. I was wondering how many other guys have really helped with the planning. Do you actually do anything? Is lip service (outside the bedroom, that is) enough? Do we really need to help? She'll still does what she wants, right? Why must we make the final choice on chair covers? Is any decision you make really the final one? What if she doesn't want to take your name? Does that make not helping easier? Thanks.

An hour later, ten replies appear on screen. Sweet. But, only one matters though.

RE: To help or not to help?
Author: SF_Bride2be-4now

Must you tell the world that you haven't helped at all?
Not happy Craig.
So not happy.

Why can't I remember to clear my browser cookies after any wedding Web session? After our own peculiar style of online romance, Deb's not in the mood to take my new haircut out for a spin. So I go out with Patrick. I feel good trash talking with Patrick, especially because he won't mention wedding, catering, honeymooning, or Deb-ing.

To cheer things up, Patrick regales me with unemployment stories. Much to the disappointment of his girlfriend, Patrick's main source of income is online sports gambling. Ah, the life of leisure.

While Patrick dissects his Atlantic Coast Conference college football picks, two women park themselves in front of us. Naturally, Patrick and I clam up and a very awkward silence falls upon the four of us.

"Please continue. It would be nice to listen to two good-looking guys talk," one of the women says.

Melodramatically, I look around the place. "Where are they?"
"Who?"

"The good-looking guys talking?" I pause for laughter, ready to downshift into some light conversation.

"You're right. Our mistake. Excuse us." They walk away.

Can life get any worse? Of course. Two losers on the other side of the bar, who were arguing the impact of Gene Roddenberry on NASA space exploration step up and buy drinks for the women. Within seconds of me shooting off my big mouth, the four of them then get huggy. I really don't care, except for the fact that I always want to be the center of attention, dance recitals and weddings aside. Even with our excessive body masses, the center of this bar scene has clearly moved from Patrick and me to those two string beans and their new slutty friends.

There's a philosophy of life that debates the merits of Abundance versus Scarcity thinking. Essentially, all people fall into one of two camps.

If you subscribe to the Abundance Principle, you believe that there is more than enough good in the world to go around. So what if your coworker gets a promotion and a raise? Good for him. You can still get one, too. And if your friend hooks up with the hottest woman in the bar? Way to go. It bodes well that you will, too.

On the other hand, backers of the Scarcity Principle believe that there is only a finite amount of good in the world. If something good happens to someone else, there's less of a chance for good to happen to you. Regardless of your ability, only so many people can get promoted. Maybe you'll have to wait until next year. And don't even think about there being more beautiful, smart, loaded women out there. Your buddy just met the last one.

For the most part, I am squarely in the Abundance camp. But with two notable exceptions: women and gambling. Thanks to my upcoming wedding, I can cross women off that list. That just leaves getting pissed off when I gamble. And a little angry when I can't find clothes that fit. And upset when my stock options aren't worth a lick. And bitter when there isn't enough time to do the things I want to do. And when . . .

Stop it. A few more days and this pressure will be gone. I'll be sipping tropical drinks in Kauai with the woman I chose to spend the rest of my life with. I remind myself that most of this stuff doesn't matter at all.

THE NAME GAME

SOME OF THE LEGAL last name options your bride can take include:

- ❥ She keeps her name as is.
- ❥ She takes your name.
- ❥ She takes your name socially, but maintains her maiden name professionally.
- ❥ She takes both names (with or without a hyphen).
- ❥ She combines both names to create a new last name (you can take that name, too).

Just make sure the proper authorities are notified.

How flexible are you? You can always take her name. Yeah, right. In fact, 42 percent of men say they'd break off the engagement if their fiancée insisted on a hyphenated last name.

Your marriage certificate supersedes all other documents as identification. Keep that in mind when you get pulled over for speeding and asked for ID. Just whip out the marriage license and say either: "I'm racing home to my wife" or "I'm racing away from my wife." You might just get a police escort.

Source: "A Nice Ring to It," *Men's Health,* June 2002

WEDDINGS ARE A BIG BUSINESS

THERE ARE ABOUT 2.1 million weddings in the United States every year.

- In the average weekend, the entire population of Charlottesville, Virginia, marries.

- In the average month, the entire population of Little Rock, Arkansas, marries.

- In the average year, the entire population of Boston, Massachusetts, marries.

Total wedding-related spending in the United States exceeds eighty billion dollars. And that doesn't include the honeymoon!

TOO BAD YOU don't have a time machine. Life was simpler (and cheaper) just a few years ago.

But don't blame increase on the cost of (throwing) rice.

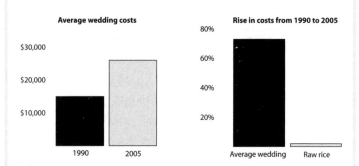

Source: Association for Wedding Professionals International (afwpi.com)
Source: 2005 American Wedding Study, The Fairchild Bridal Group
Source: International Rice Research Institute (irri.org)

WHY WHITE?

IT IS THE bride's veil, and not a white dress, that symbolizes virginity. Therefore, any bride should feel free to wear white. However, it is considered inappropriate for a woman who has already been married to wear a veil.

The white gown is actually a symbol of joy. Early Greeks and Romans wore white for special feasts, including weddings, births, and other celebrations. They would even paint their bodies white on the evening of wedding ceremonies. While white symbolizes innocents and purity, blue is the color of true love and fidelity.

In Asian cultures, brides wear red, which symbolizes good luck. In Japan, purple, the color of love, is used to accent kimonos.

If you thought buying one dress was one too many, Indian brides often wear a red sari for the ceremony and change into a white outfit for the reception.

WHEN THE BACHELORETTE'S AWAY, THE MICE DO WEDDING CHORES.

> One of the best things about marriage
> is that it gets young people to bed at a decent hour.
> (M. M. Musselman)

I REALLY HOPE my job works out. Not because I want to rule the world. But because I want to have an extra few bucks in my (correction, our) bank account. That'll help start the marriage off right. After all, I am paying for two. Someday three. Maybe four. Hopefully not five. But you never know. My "boys" might be excellent swimmers.

Although, if our sex life continues on the path it's taking, we'll be stuck on two for quite some time. But I have faith in our sex life picking up. It really has only one way to go. On the other hand, Deb's become very concerned with bringing children into a society that's changed for the worse.

"There's too much destruction in the world. Why subject new lives to all this negativity?" Deb questions.

"I want a captive audience for my material."

"What are you talking about?"

"First, the physical stuff. Silly faces. Jumping around.

Then, simple jokes. Chicken. Road. Egg. The usual. Finally, the hard stuff. Ironic observations. Self-deprecation."

"Stand-up act aside, I just don't know."

"No kids? Two words. Deal breaker."

"I know. I'll breed for you. Don't panic."

"Don't forget our baby starter kit."

"I know. And you'll pick the breed. Don't panic."

Before having kids, I want a dog. Not a "look, it's a cute, furry rodent-like thing" dog, but a "look out, you're going to get slobbered on, jumped on, and harassed to throw a ball every waking moment" dog. Besides being man's best friend, my dog will be perfect baby training. We'll have schedules to keep. Mouths to feed. Things to buy. Maybe I should have gotten a dog earlier. Could a dog have been perfect wedding-planning training as well?

Now that our brief discussion on family planning is over (read: I won one!), we focus on today's main agenda item: Deb's bachelorette party (read: Deb's time to get back at me for winning one).

✧

DEB'S BACHELORETTE PARTY is also in Tahoe. But I doubt they'll venture to Reno. On the off chance they do, I doubt they'll be going to the same places I went. Please don't go to the same places. Please. Even though our first date included a heart-to-heart talk on Deb's willingness to go to strip joints, we have never gone together. No need to let her see my ugly side. I'll psych myself up for that at some point, but I would hate for our strip joint experience to start by her seeing a black-and-white photo of me with the caption "Do not let this predator in."

Her party is turning out to be much smaller than originally planned. At this point, Deb is tired of the fuss and formalities of the pre-wedding and just wants to get to the fuss and formalities of the wedding. As your average male hypocrite, I fully support her desire to keep the party low-key. Exhausted from work and still recovering from my escapades with Patrick last night, I only manage to send Deb off with a hug and kiss.

"That's all?" Deb asks.

"Do you need money?" I am well trained.

"Sure, but how about a bigger good-bye? Maybe even two good-byes?"

"Will you settle for a few welcome-backs?"

"I might."

"Be good."

"I might."

And the house is mine again. But this time I know she's coming back. At least I think she will. There are not many gifts a fiancée can give to her husband-to-be better than forty-eight hours of uninterrupted peace and quiet. Has it been long enough to justify a San Francisco bachelor party reunion? I find myself feeling differently about strip joints. Excitement? Nope. Pleasure? Nope. Shyness? Nope. Guilt? Yup. Scummy guilt? Not really, although I probably should. More like money guilt. I think it's better to save a few bucks and not put out a call to arms.

This must be temporary. We've had a lot of expenses these past few months, but once the honeymoon is over, we'll be back in the black. Or will we? I frantically call Drew and ask if this is what responsibility is like. Like he knows. Which is precisely why I called him.

Maybe I should just settle for a few affordable pay-per-view movies. Even this doesn't feel right. I am trapped. Deb's taking over some bill-paying responsibilities and I'd rather not have "eXXXtreme Block of Sin 2" showing up on our first cable bill as a married couple. Should I tape it for the honeymoon? Would that be crossing the scummy line? I better delete "Where the Boys Aren't 8" from my Netflix queue.

It's just me, a pizza, two *Simpsons,* and a stack of thank-you cards. An ever-growing evil that has been haunting me for weeks. But before putting pen to paper, I jot down a few standard phrases that'll let me say the same thing to everyone without really saying the same thing to everyone.

We can't wait to use _____.

_____ is going to be helpful for years to come.

Looking forward to breaking out the _____ when you visit.

If only I could say what I am really feeling.

_____ is very thoughtful, especially since Deb forced me to put it on the registry. I hope I won't be using your gift while staring at our same, tiny TV because not enough of my friends had the balls to kick in on the present I really want. Correction, the present I really need. I'm looking forward to bringing out your gift the two times you'll visit and telling you how I couldn't imagine living my life without it. See you at the wedding!

NO, THANK *YOU,*
A SIMPLE THANK-YOU NOTE TEMPLATE.

HERE'S WHAT YOU SHOULD SAY

Dear (Name of gift giver),
Thank you so much for the (Gift). We are happy that you were able to attend the wedding and appreciate your generosity. We can't wait to (Activity you'll use gift for) with the (Gift). It'll come in handy for many years to come.

Love,
(Your name) and (Your fiancée's name)

HERE'S WHAT YOU PROBABLY WANT TO SAY

Dear (Name of gift giver),
 Thank you so much for the (Gift). We are happy that you were able to attend the wedding and will think of you the (Number of times you'll use the gift) times we (Activity you'll use gift for) with the (Gift). I am looking forward to the hours of fun trying to cram your (Adjective describing gift) gift into what little closet space we have until you come over and then spend yet more hours digging deep to retrieve it just to prove that we like your gift.
 Of course, a (Name of gift you really wanted) would have been a better gift for me. That was what I asked for, but was shot down by (Your fiancée's name). I could always

return the (Gift) for the (Monetary value of gift) and apply it toward the (Name of gift you really wanted). However, I would probably need to use some of the proceeds of your gift return to start a legal defense fund.

(Depending on your relation to gift giver)

If relative: Love,

If friend: Sincerely,

If stranger/relative you just met at wedding: Who are you again?

(Your name) and (Your fiancée's name)

P.S. We are still registered at (Name of registry store), just in case you win the lottery or come down with a case of generosity.

■

HOME ALONE? TIPS TO MAKE HER NIGHT OUT EVEN MORE PLEASURABLE:

- Clean your house.
- Clean her house.
- Leave a few love notes around her place (also good to mark your territory if her night becomes *too* good).
- Prepare a honeymoon-themed greeting for her return.
- Get her car's oil changed.
- Cook her favorite meal or dessert (even if it's whipped cream and you).
- Buy flowers and actually put them in a vase (with water).
- Record her favorite show (even if you have to watch the ballgame on a smaller TV).
- Bid on the one collective figurine she's missing from her display cabinet.
- Call her mom just to say thanks.
- Pay a bill of hers.
- Stay out of her underwear drawer.
- Organize her tabloid magazine collection.
- Shave your back.

FORGET THE ENVIRONMENT. NEVER RECYCLE PORN.

A man in love is incomplete until he is married.
Then he is finished.
(Zsa Zsa Gabor)

WHAT'S DEB DOING at her bachelorette party? It's probably a toss between a spa pampering with the ladies and kicking last night's Rambo-hunk to the curb. Knowing her crew, I doubt I have to defend my turf. Which will let me save the zebra thong until it really counts. Why ruin the honeymoon?

I can't avoid my to-do list any longer. As lame as it sounds, I think I have perfected the art of combining errands with exercising. I just strap on my backpack and run out the front door. First, the sporting goods store (snorkel). Loop around to the post office (my wonderfully written thank-you notes from our engagement and early wedding gifts). Then, the camera store (waterproof case). Finally, the grocery store (nourishment). This highly efficient approach might have patent potential. Maybe even the start of a whole new workout program. Good-bye, Tae Bo. Hello, Exershop. So long, Spinning. Meet Purchasising. Forget the Cardio Kick. Welcome to the Plastic Punchout.

Properly filling the backpack after each stop is essential to the program. It's nothing any Safeway clerk can't tell you. But does he or she have the foresight to apply their bagging technique to a life-changing system? From experience, I have learned that one must not buy eggs, carbonated beverages, or excessively large fruit on the To-Do Skidoo program. Cans go on the bottom, snacks on top. And keep hot stuff away from the body.

Done before noon. Five miles. Two hundred bucks. Forty dollars a mile. Fifty cents a calorie. Not bad.

✧

HOME IS EMPTY. My heart saddens. Tripping over a pile of laundry makes that moment pass. Our apartment is a mess. This man's job is never done.

I must be able to box Deb's bridal magazines by now. We're way beyond any of the how-to articles and if not, I'm sure she has a few hidden stashes somewhere. Since our engagement, piles of wedding literature have been collecting throughout the house. Ironically, most of them are dated well before I proposed. I first discovered those while cleaning—only six months after we started dating. It was bad enough that the discovery was during my semi-annual cushion-flipping day, but finding a year's worth of *Modern Bride* cut what remaining stump of manhood I had right off.

✧

"HONEY, CAN YOU help me out?" I innocently asked, hoping for a good excuse, or at least a good apology.

Deb replied from the bedroom, "If you can't flip the cushions on your own, maybe you should go to the gym more."

"I flipped. Actually, I'm flipped," I said pointing to the magazines.

"You weren't meant to see those," Deb professed.

"Well from the dog ears, Post-Its, and pen marks, I know you've been reading them."

"A girl can dream, can't she?"

"Any other dreams I should know about before I look in your underwear drawer?"

"Just this one. You okay?"

"Well the couches just got more comfortable. I guess that lessens the blow."

Deb was never so embarrassed. Since my mind was already made up about us and where we were headed, I was able to appreciate the cuteness of her actions. But there was absolutely no need to fill Deb in on my intentions just yet. Watching my woman squirm was a real treat.

✧

AFTER GATHERING THE bedroom, bathroom, and living room magazines and a few random issues that found their way under the couch again, I make one big pile. Four feet high. The apartment never looked bigger. That might seem like a lot of reading material, but dozens of trees were sacrificed for only a few original articles about planning a perfect wedding. The remaining 99 percent of pages are consumed by seemingly thousands of dress, makeup, vacation, and various feminine product advertisements.

I won't dare toss the pile in the recycling bin without Deb's final approval. All I can do is get them neatly arranged for one final heave-ho. Deb might want to donate the magazines to a recently engaged friend or someone trying to push her man over the edge. I certainly can't help in this department. Unless Drew needs kindling for his fireplace. Or Rick hasn't trained his puppy yet. Maybe we should make an end table out of them? More like an eight-piece sectional sofa.

Tit for tat, I feel compelled to toss some tit. I dig into my vault and gather some of my magazines and movies that I have been collecting over the past few years. As far as I know, Deb hasn't discovered them. While they aren't specifically about weddings, I remember a few virgins dressed in white in some of the spreads.

I don't neatly stack my collection for Deb to decide its fate. I know exactly what to do: triple-bag, hermetically seal, and throw them down the trash chute. Then a quick scan of the place to make sure any "Call Me," "Subscribe Now," or "Amazing She-Males on DVD" response cards haven't fallen out. All's clear. It feels good to make a fresh start. For a while. I know myself well enough to predict that eventually they'll be back. And by then, with one glace at my ring finger, the convenience store clerk will have stopped looking at me as a pathetic single guy and start looking at me as a really pathetic married guy.

Being knee-deep in porn makes me feel a bit nostalgic. I rummage through another stash of mine: old pictures and letters from ex-girlfriends. It's obvious. Deb's the cutest. Smartest. Funniest. Three for three.

DEB STILL HASN'T called from her bachelorette party. Good for her. She shouldn't. I wish I could do that. Hell, I wish I could resist calling her right now.

"Anything good?" I innocently ask. My apron must be tied too tight around my housedress.

"I am not supposed to tell," Deb coyly replies.

"Was he bigger than me?" I strongly object.

"No one's bigger than you," she politely demurs.

"You really know how to confuse the issue."

"Wait until you add me to your American Express. Then you'll experience confusion."

NEED TO DROP A FEW POUNDS?
A FEW INCHES?
A FEW FEET?

NO TIME LIKE the present. To give you a clue as to where you stand and what you can do to lose that gut, here are some handy formulas. You'll even burn at least five calories just doing the math. As long as you drop that potato chip before proceeding.

Body Mass Index
Body Mass Index (BMI) is an indicator of total body fat.

$$= (weight\ in\ pounds\ / \ (height\ in\ inches * height\ in\ inches)) * 703$$

What does your BMI mean?

Below 18.5	You're underweight (buddy up with Ben & Jerry's)
18.5-24.9	You're normal (don't change a thing, regardless of what your fiancée says)
25.0-29.9	You're overweight (consider skipping a meal or two)
30.0 and above	You're obese (remember, those elastic tux waists only stretch so far)

Daily maintenance calories

Your daily maintenance calories is a measure of how many calories you need to consume to maintain your current weight. If your goal is to lose weight (1 pound per week), subtract 500 calories per day from this result. If the goal is to gain weight (1 pound per week), add 500 calories per day.

$$= ((\text{height in centimeters} * 5) + (\text{weight in kilograms} * 13.7)$$
$$-(\text{age in years} * 6.8) + 66) * \text{your activity level}$$

Activity level values:

1.25	Not active (your bedsores have bedsores)
1.30	Lightly active (you've driven past your gym recently)
1.50	Moderately active (you've parked at your gym recently)
1.70	Very active (the gym knows who you are)
2.00	Hardcore active (the gym is named after you)

Calories burned for common activities

Is it better to ski or golf, calorically speaking? Can you actually lose weight shopping for ice cream? Can you provide your fiancée with a real medical reason to have sex with you? Here's a simple way to measure the burn and the results for an average guy:

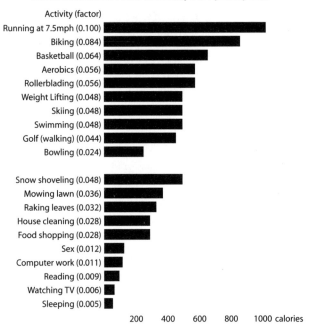

= (weight in pounds * workout duration in minutes * exercise factor)

Calories burned on a 1-hour workout by a 170-pound person

Activity (factor)

Activity (factor)	
Running at 7.5mph (0.100)	
Biking (0.084)	
Basketball (0.064)	
Aerobics (0.056)	
Rollerblading (0.056)	
Weight Lifting (0.048)	
Skiing (0.048)	
Swimming (0.048)	
Golf (walking) (0.044)	
Bowling (0.024)	
Snow shoveling (0.048)	
Mowing lawn (0.036)	
Raking leaves (0.032)	
House cleaning (0.028)	
Food shopping (0.028)	
Sex (0.012)	
Computer work (0.011)	
Reading (0.009)	
Watching TV (0.006)	
Sleeping (0.005)	

200   400   600   800   1000 calories

Disclaimer: This information is provided for educational purposes only and is not intended to be a substitute for professional medical advice or diagnosis of specific medical conditions. You should seek prompt professional medical attention if you have a particular concern about your health or specific symptoms.

THINGS TO DUMP
BEFORE YOUR HOUSEHOLDS MERGE,
OR AT LEAST PUT IN COLD STORAGE.

- Porn.
- Suggestive photos of you.
- Suggestive photos of ex-girlfriends.
- Suggestive photos of women from any Web site that begins with "hot."
- Blow-up furniture.
- Blow-up roommates.
- Outdoor furniture used indoors.
- Any furniture with more stain than fabric showing.
- Ten-year-old shirts.
- Five-year-old underwear.
- Anything hanging on your wall without a frame.
- Collection of *How to Pick Up Women* books.
- Combination alarm clock/sexual partner-counter on your nightstand.
- The one pot you have in your kitchen.
- The one cereal bowl you have in your sink.
- Anything with neon.
- Random toothbrush collection in your bathroom drawer.
- Random key collection in your kitchen drawer.
- Random empty collection (e.g., bottles, cans, shot glasses, bullet shells) anywhere in the house.
- Everything in your refrigerator.
- All your linens (especially if you don't know what linens are).

4

NO TIME LIKE THE PRESENT. BECAUSE THERE'S NO TIME LEFT.

One week to go

New To-Do's

Pack your bags.

> It's not what you think. Or if you failed miserably at helping her plan the wedding, it is what you think. Take a few moments and pack a change of clothes for after the reception and all your new honeymoon attire. Doing this early will ensure you have time for some last-minute purchases. You can't have enough flower-print shirts and boat shoes.

Arrange move to new home and change-of-address form, if necessary.

> If there's any moving to be done, do it now to make it easier when you get back from your honeymoon. Throw out the garbage (translation: anything your fiancée says is the "old you"), box your stuff, and coordinate the movers (or the U-Haul truck, if you are a do-it-yourselfer).

Pick up tuxedo.

> Try on your tux to make sure all the measurements were correct. Or if your weight swung one way or the other, there's enough time to alter the outfit. Also, follow up with everyone in your wedding party, including fathers, to make sure they pick up their tuxedos as well. Nothing ruins a wedding faster than a group of guys who look like they picked their formalwear from Goodwill.

Upgrade personal hygiene.

> Time's running out. While you probably won't drop a few inches around your waist or get those six-pack abs she really wants, there are things you can do to be more presentable during your wedding (and beyond). Get a haircut. Floss more often.

to-do's

Sleep a bit longer. And a few last-minute workouts and stomach crunches wouldn't hurt, either.

OLD TO-DO'S LEFT TO DO

	How late am I?
Shop for honeymoon clothes	2 months
Pick up wedding rings	2 months
Verify honeymoon plans	2 weeks
Pour your heart out (write vows, speeches, and toasts)	2 weeks
Pick up license	1 week

Take 548

THE NEXT STEVEN SPIELBERGO.

Before marriage, a man declares that he would lay down his life to serve you; after marriage, he won't even lay down his newspaper to talk to you.
(Helen Rowland)

I MUST BE a masochist. It's a week before the wedding and here I am, running a one-man production trying to shoot a short film. And for whom? Me? Must I need my fifteen minutes of fame now? My mom? She'll probably watch whatever I make until her DVD player burns up. For Deb? Not really, but it was an idea of hers that sparked me. She went to a woman's book club and suggested that I make a short about a men's book club. But instead of an Oprah book being discussed, the gentlemen would debate the merits of porn magazines.

Why now versus filming in a few months? The only thing I can think of is that I've been overcome by a sudden urge to create something to leave as my pre-married legacy. Before my identity blurs, babies start to cry, and I'm drooling over the Porsche I can't afford because I didn't take this first step toward Hollywood. Plus, there's a local film contest going on.

First prize won't put a down payment on the Porsche but would probably cover the first tank of gas. And, at current prices, still means decent money being given away.

None of my friends arrive on time for filming. What if they show up late to the wedding? Deb wouldn't have a cow—she'd pass the whole herd. Where are these people?

As I check my binder for the twentieth time, something big hits me. I count up how much time and energy I spent preparing for this project. The writing. The research. The planning. All in painstaking detail. The people. The equipment. The directions. The snacks.

Ouch. I am a planner. In fact, I am a great planner. And I am worse than pond scum.

Deb has done the same planning with the wedding. Only with two big differences. She's producing an entire weekend, not just an ill-conceived five-minute movie. And she wouldn't have dragged her heels, like me, to lend a hand. Nor went out of her way to avoid helping. What stopped me from doing those little extras for her? It isn't enough to listen occasionally and whip out the credit card every now and then. She deserves more. I wish it wasn't so late to make a difference. Make a decision. Take an interest. Pick a bouquet. It'll be years before I'll ever live this down.

But enough about my misdoings. Right now, I deserve a friend who knows how to tell time, if not memorize a script and deliver his line on cue. Where are they? I shouldn't complain. They are always good to me in a pinch, wedding support aside. We've had our moments. Mostly girl-free moments, but a moment is a moment.

✧

THE BEST OF these moments happened when Drew and I roomed together in school. We would host a barbeque every Friday night. And every barbeque tended to have the same theme: sausage fest. And I don't mean the grilling kind. We finally bet each other as to when the first female would visit our place. Four months. Not bad. I expected four years. But then again, someone has to read the electric meter.

I TRY TO finish the filming by a decent hour, but a great deal is left to get done. I block actors. Adjust lights. Rewrite dialogue. Push a grocery cart (my low-budget dolly). Totally fun, but totally irrelevant in the current scheme of things. Guilt isn't just rearing its ugly head. It has climbed on my shoulders and doing the Macarena (did I agree to this one at the wedding?). Enough. I've gone through eight tapes and five camera batteries. I think I have enough footage that it'll take me the whole honeymoon to edit. (Just kidding. I'm not that stupid.)

"It's a wrap!"

I love doing this. Plus I know my boundaries. I don't expect to be the next Hitchcock or Wells. I'd be ecstatic to direct *Dude, I Still Can't Find My Car XXIII*. Not sure if it's in the cards for me, but I guarantee that my son will have a video camera in his crib way before he puts on a baseball glove. Especially since he'll have my athletic abilities, or lack thereof.

✧

I RACE TO pick up Deb's ring from Tiffany's. It needed to get resized a bit, and she's expecting it before getting back home. I can't disappoint her on this one. There will be plenty of other disappointments to come. For instance: my ring has yet to arrive. Who knew that cheapplatinum.com would have such a slow order fulfillment process. I inquire at the San Francisco Tiffany's if they have a band in my size just in case.

"Size ten. Of course sir, that's our model size."

I must have blocked that little fact out. "Wonderful."

✧

DEB BREAKS DOWN the minute she walks in the door. No time for her to compliment my cleaning or question her magazine stack in the middle of the living room. "Are you sure we have enough appetizers?"

"Yes."

"Why did we pick Vegas? Why did you pick Vegas? Who the hell plans a wedding in Vegas?"

"Easy, sweetie."

"What about the weather?"

"It's a desert. I think we'll be fine. What did those girls do to you?"

There's not much I can do to assuage her, except call the hotel and order a dozen heat lamps. And tomorrow, I'll call our guests and ask them to wear layers at the wedding.

"Will the ceremony be a joke?"

"Why?"

"It's just puff with no substance."

"It'll be great. You did a great job."

"What about you? Why didn't you help at all?"

Danger, Will Robinson. Danger. "I didn't want to ruin anything." Was that the right thing to say?

"It's not going to be good."

"Seriously, what happened this weekend? Who said what?"

"Nothing happened."

"Is that the problem? Do you want me to take you to Chippendales? I'll do it. Just don't expect me to tip that much. Even if he's packing a whopper."

"Are we too different?"

"What?"

"Do you want to marry a Catholic?"

"Catholic. Jew. Atheist. Martian. You could be anything."

What a bad case of the wedding worries. Maybe she's just frustrated after having been with gyrating guys all weekend. We should have had sex before she left.

Dutifully, I shake my booty and pulsate to a Lexus commercial playing on TV. Not ideal, but what's a panicked groom to do? Regardless, it's too late to stir any amorous feelings.

"I hope you're practicing for our dance?" she deflects, half in tears, half in jest.

"Come on, baby. I'll give you some money to stuff in my undies."

"Any money you give me, I'm keeping."

She's coming back.

"And we must do something about your tighty-whities. Time to grow up and wear some boxers."

Welcome home, Deb.

Seeing that we won't be getting physical, I resort to more verbal intercourse hoping to keep the cheer alive as we climb into bed. I start with tender foreplay ("Everything will be fabulous. I can feel it."). Followed by a slow cadence of affirmations ("I can't wait for the wedding. Everyone will love it."). And finish her off with powerful pulse of ecstasy-inducing excitement ("You'll look amazing. You look amazing. You'll always look amazing."). Three minutes of hard-core talking. Whew. I am spent. If only I could last that long normally. As usual, I leave Deb sorely unsatisfied, but asleep in my arms.

YOUR SCAMMING DAYS ARE OVER, BUT YOU CAN STILL HELP YOUR SINGLE FRIENDS OUT.

HOPEFULLY YOU'VE LOADED your wedding with eligible singles. Your pals (and your bride's pals) expect this, so don't disappoint them. To assist with ranking their best options, make copies of this form and hand them out at the wedding.

This is equal opportunity scamming at its best—the form works for women and men. Let the games begin!

Wedding Scamming Score Card

Your Marital Status Check only one box.	☐ Single: 0 points ☐ Dating: -2 points ☐ Married: -5 points	**1**	
Target's Marital Status Check only one box.	☐ Happily married, with spouse: 0 points ☐ Married, but alone tonight: 1 point ☐ Dating, with date: 1 point ☐ Dating, but alone: 2 points ☐ Single, with friends: 3 points ☐ Single, and lonely: 5 points	**2**	
Wedding Experience	1 point for every wedding target has been TO this year	**3**	
	2 points for every wedding target has been IN this year	**4**	
Alcohol Consumption	1 point for every 2 drinks you have had already	**5**	
	1 point for every drink target has had already	**6**	
Wedding/Hotel Info	5 points if wedding is out of town	**7**	
	5 points if reception is in your hotel this evening	**8**	
	-2 points if you are sharing a room with other people	**9**	
	1 point if target needs a ride somewhere	**10**	
Ceremony Info	2 points if target cried during ceremony	**11**	
	1 point if target is in the wedding party	**12**	
Target's Age Check only one box.	☐ 18 - 25: 1 point ☐ 26 - 35: 2 points ☐ 36 - 45: 1 point	**13**	
Speaking Terms	1 point if you have already talked with target	**14**	
	1 bonus point if target has laughed at your jokes	**15**	
Attractiveness	2 points if you are good looking	**16**	
	-2 points if your target is good looking	**17**	
Target's Value	0 - 5: Pass on this one. 6 - 10: Make a move early to see if target bites. Beware, you might only score a hardy handshake. 11 - 15: Getting warmer. Keep an eye on this one. 16 - 20: Not a sure thing, but the gods are smiling on you. 21+: What are you waiting for???	**18**	

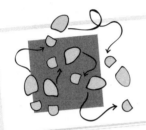

IT TAKES TWO TO TANGO. THREE, IF ONE DOESN'T KNOW HOW TO DANCE.

Love is blind, but marriage restores its sight.
(Georg Christoph Lichtenberg)

I SPEND THREE hours confirming hotel reservations. Before the wedding. After the wedding. At the Oakland airport. In Kauai. For us. For my parents. For my groomsmen. For my getaway. The only hotel I am worried about is Patrick's. Tempting fate, he opted for a cheaper room at the other end of the Vegas Strip. It's not the long walk between our hotels I fear. It's the lure of the 99-cent buffets along the way.

Our honeymoon hotel convinces me to upgrade. There are eighteen different room types to choose from. I initially booked the Partial Parking, Partial Tennis Court View, Ground Floor, Half Studio choice. Who's going to have the time to look at the view?

But they're right; we should have the cliché self-portrait of the happy honeymooners couple on their balcony overlooking the ocean. I'm such a sucker for romance. I agree to take the Full Tennis Court View, Second Floor, Junior Suite that you can see the ocean if there's a strong enough wind to blow the palm trees down. I even order a welcome basket of flowers, tropical fruit, and mini-bottle of champagne for our arrival. If all this doesn't make Deb amorous, I honestly don't know what will.

I hope to apply the "we're on our honeymoon, give us free stuff" line to the fullest extent possible on this trip. This is the one time to semi-legitimately schmooze our way into flying first class, being served free desserts, getting extra time on the Ferris wheel, and a whole host of other goodies. I usually hate asking, but I'm going to make an exception. Deb can flash her ring around while I grovel for freebies so the clerks won't think I am a complete cheapskate. Only a half-skate who broke the bank on his lady. Maybe I should get that printed on my credit card? "In hoc since 2000."

✧

A FEW WEEKS ago, I suggested we should have table themes at the reception and not just boring numbers. Deb was skeptical about these themes clashing with our overall motif (clean and elegant). I don't mind the potential of clashing. I mind the reality of bankruptcy. Our invitations cost a fortune, and when I found out that name cards were going to be almost as much, I planned on putting my computer skills and company's ten-thousand-dollar color printer to good use.

Each table will be named after a memorable event in our lives. The centerpieces will tell a little story written about each event. It's not being cheap. It's being creative and sentimental.

I'm psyched to tell Deb about my brainstorming. "Come on. At a minimum, it would be a conversation starter."

"I guess."

"And maybe we'll do a trivia contest. Find out how much people know about us. We can test them on the bus ride back to the hotels. Casino chips as prizes?"

"Save that for our fiftieth anniversary party. Are you done with the cards yet?"

"You'll see tonight."

I dig deep for a few festive, upbeat memories. If I restrict myself to the past few months, I don't think Deb would appreciate "Three AM screaming fest," "No sex June," "Raft-o-rama," or "Psychoanalysis session number two."

It takes a few hours, a few drinks and a few hundred attempts, but I come up with some winners:

SFO Jetway: Where we first met . . . Craig made the first of many foot-in-mouth comments, but thankfully recovered enough to get a first date from the lovely Deb.

Empire Tap Room, Palo Alto: Where we had our first date . . . coincidentally, at the same table where Deb was dumped three months prior. Her nail marks and tear stains were still there, but wiped away by Craig's affection.

Monkey Bar, Costa Rica: Where we had our fifth date . . . and where passion lit the sky. Or was it banana daiquiris that filled our bloodstream?

New Year's Eve, San Francisco: Where we got engaged . . . all caught on tape for evidence (er, proof).

Glover's Reef, Belize: Where we spent a week on our own private island . . . and Craig tried to apply his Gilligan skills to cook coconut stew. Luckily, Deb upgraded us to the "food and shelter inclusive" package before we arrived.

Las Vegas: Where we will get married . . . and hopefully be dealt a royal flush at video poker (but not because your gifts were so cheap).

Kauai, Hawaii: Where we are going on our honeymoon . . . to soak up the sun and more banana daiquiris.

For a grand total of eleven dollars, our table cards are done, and if I must say so myself (which I think I'll have to do), they look good. Double-sided, black-matted. Only the best. I call Deb with a progress report.

"Cute," she says.

"So we can cancel the other ones?" I ask.

"Which ones?"

"The ones you have in reserve."

"How did you know?"

"You think I'm all looks and no brains?"

"I never thought you were all looks. This is all about saving money, isn't it?"

"No. It's about sharing our happy times with everyone."

"Hope you lied better on those happy cards."

WE MAKE OUR way to the dance studio for our second private lesson. Also known as my last chance to become Fred Astaire. Or at least Felipe, a backup dancer for N'Sync. I didn't think private lesson number two could be worse than private lesson number one, but apparently I underestimate my ability to inflict pain on myself and others with my feet. Why can't we go back to dancing a simple box step the entire four minutes? That would be too easy. I must "glide" around the room. Head high. Back arched. Arms locked. Knees bent. Just like golf. Too bad I score in the hundreds and lose balls by the dozens when I play golf. My excuses fly.

"I just need the right shoes."

"Is there a video we can take home?"

"Can't everyone dance the first song with us?"

"What first song?" Deb cuts me down.

We still haven't decided on our wedding song. I did my best to replace listening to Howard Stern every morning with as many lite radio stations I could stand. While I haven't found the perfect song, I now know exactly how Don Blue (in The Morning) enjoys his coffee.

Deb takes a more pragmatic approach and brings thirty CDs to the dance studio, hoping something will feel right during our lesson. Alas, nothing feels right. I am a mess. I can't remember moves from two minutes ago. I'm downgraded to "remedial status," and have to dance with Serge more than with Deb. He does have a certain charm. And he knows how to make me feel like the man I want to be. Note to self: have Serge talk to Deb before we leave.

We settle on a lovely Sinatra song ("Fly Me to the Moon"). Not too short. Not too long. Enough spin time for Deb to grab the attention of our guests.

"Some students bring their teacher to the wedding. For comfort," Serge kindly mentions.

Would it be kosher for Serge to lurk behind my parents whispering "slow, slow, quick, quick" to me? How much would it cost for him to gain twenty pounds, dye his hair brown, stand on his toes, and step in for me? Flying Serge to Vegas sounds tempting. "Thanks, but I can do it."

"Of course you can," Serge offers.

"Stick to dancing, Serge. Your acting's awful."

✧

THE FINAL RESULTS from the last of the Win Your Dream Wedding contests we applied for arrive today. So far, we're zero for eight contests, which includes the *Today Show, Good Morning America, Bride's,* and the *Kansas Morning Star.* This could be the one. We made it to the final five (out of three thousand entries). Deb's rooting for us to win the major appliances. I'm hoping for the six-page photo spread.

Deb had a foolproof contest plan, and this fool almost won it. She figured brides-to-be would be the only ones writing the entries. After all, who else reads these magazines? Why not have our entry written by the groom? As usual, she was right. It worked like a charm. I was sincere, loving, and spoke from my heart when I told them what makes our relationship work:

From the moment we met, our lives changed. And over time, we strengthen every one of the powerful bonds that bind our relationship. While there are way too many bonds to count, a few stand out as so fundamental to our being, that they enable us to act with one mind, body, and spirit as we prepare for a new life together.

We finish each other's thoughts, on any subject.

We laugh together, all the time.

We never take each other for granted, learning with every word.

We take leaps together, and equally.

We are at complete ease, open to communicating anything.

We discover lots of scary little things about ourselves, for endless amusement.

I can really lay it on thick when pressed. And we were charming during the personal interviews. According to Deb, who researched the past five winners, the only thing that would stop us is that we didn't have enough tragedies in our lives. A sad-sack couple could easily trump my flowery prose. Throughout the interviews, we tried to argue our not-so-bad-life case. The Internet collapse hurt our take-out budget. Our family's disappointment in us living together drove Deb to Botox. We could never agree on the same television show.

And the winner is . . . not us. Apparently, the lucky couple had a few more believable obstacles to overcome. She became deathly ill while working on relief efforts in some third-world country. He was in medical school, volunteering time, and wound up treating her. After three years of no contact, they found each other and he asked for her hand (the correct one, unlike me). Not bad. All Deb and I have is a corny Web site and a drunken memory of how I proposed. Note to self: cancel the stop-payments on our vendor checks. Guess we're paying for this shindig after all.

MARITAL SEX,
ISN'T THAT AN OXYMORON?

THE GOOD NEWS is that you could be having sex more after you're married:

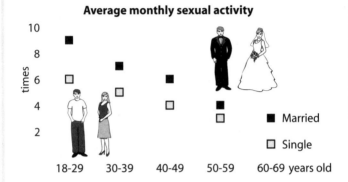

Average monthly sexual activity

Source: "Sex After Marriage," GMA/ABC News, 2/21/01

The bad news is that you might not last as long.

Thirty percent of women who don't live with a man say that the last time they had sex, it lasted for more than an hour. Only 13 percent of women in live-in relationships and 8 percent of wives claimed that as well. But is this good news, too? After all, you can get back to watching *The Simpsons* faster.

Source: health.discovery.com

It's okay if you aren't that skilled. She probably won't know the difference. A third of adult Americans have sex only a few times a year or not at all. The median number of sexual partners over a lifetime for American men is six. For women, it's two. Plus more than 80 percent of Americans had only one sexual partner or no partner in an average year. Just 3 percent of women and men had five or more partners in an average year.

And don't be too worried about her cheating. Seventy-five percent of married men and 85 percent of married women say they remain faithful. And to top it off, studies have found that monogamous couples tend to have the most sex and are happiest with their sex lives.

Source: *The University of Chicago Chronicle,* October 13, 1994

Want to optimize your sex life? Live in sin for as long as possible, but when you do marry, have kids quickly. Or just cut to the chase by getting your girlfriend pregnant and elope.

Average annual sexual activity

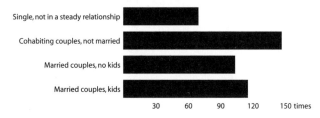

Source: 1997 Durex Global Sex Survey

And while her parents might object, the times are a changing: over half of all marriages are preceded by the couple living together. Just don't be the guy who had to get the ultimatum after living together for years. And years. And years. But if you are, say you're a slow eater, too.

Source: "The State of Our Unions: 2005," National Marriage Project, Rutgers University

THE SPEECHLESS BEST MAN AND THE EVEN MORE SPEECHLESS GROOM.

You can't change a man, no-ways.
By the time his Mummy turns him loose and
he takes up with some innocent woman and marries her,
he's what he is.
(Marjorie Kinnan Rawlings)

MY BROTHER—AND best man—Jon calls at work. He's usually too busy with law school to give me the time of day. What a treat.

"I'm concerned about the wedding toast," Jon starts with. What a trick. "This is a tough one, with you being best man and all," I reply.

"I need to know more about Deb."

"And whose fault is that?"

"Well, yours."

He's got me. Being five years apart made sharing the same interests difficult, TV viewings aside. The last thing I want to do is tell Deb that I have to find a pinch-speaker because my brother lacks a few personally felt adjectives to describe her. It's way too late to change the course of wedding history.

I chose Jon to be my best man because he's family. And family is important to me. Even though, according to some, my moving three thousand miles from home showed an "utter disregard for family." (Thank you, Aunt Sarah. Can't wait to see you at the wedding.)

"Whatever you want to know about Deb, I'll tell you," I offer.

"Okay, what's your favorite thing about Deb?" he asked. Did he not get my latest newsletter? The one headlined with "My Favorite Things About Deb"?

"She lets me make fun of her."

"That's romantic?"

"Hey. She makes fun of me, too."

"All right, 'a match made in heaven.' That's a good start."

"Just wait. After you lift your head out of the law books and find the woman of your dreams, you might have a hard time describing her, too."

"Okay, but I think I'll prescreen for comedic flaws."

"Lovable quirks."

"Sustained. But I'll stick with the law books for now."

We end the conversation with some well-thought-out brotherly advice from me. "At the wedding, just act like a cruise director. Make sure the guests get around without difficulty and they don't pester me with too many questions. . . ." He's silent, so I succumb to (what I think is) genius. "Wait, even better: Consider me a sequestered juror who can't face too many sidebars or interrogatories." At least I read his legal newsletters.

✧

I'm surrounded during an all-hands company meeting. For amusement, I check to see who is wearing a wedding ring. Not a pretty sight. With few exceptions, the men seemed older, larger, and bitterer. Am I just projecting? They do seem to be the more successful ones, but they also have to divide their salary in half. And, if you mess up the first time and try again, in half again. And for the poor soul standing next to me, in half once more.

Am I about to make a major switch? Will the married crowd accept me? Will I accept them? Do women check out a man's ring finger as much as men do with women? Will I become instantly more attractive?

Will I always wear my ring? Uncle Bob doesn't. My dad doesn't. I can always cite family precedence.

If I don't wear my ring, should I expect Deb to change her name? Do most married women change their name? Will it be a big deal if Deb doesn't change hers? Is she not fully committing to me by keeping her family name?

At least our kids will be Michaels . . . right?

Does any of this really matter? Is it hot in here or what?

"Where's your ring?" Deb greets me, dispensing with the pleasantries.

So much for not being branded for life. "I swear, it's en route. I'll track the shipment."

"You're killing me, you know that? There's not much I asked you to do."

"I know."

"You agree having both rings is important for the success of the ceremony?"

"Of course."

"So it'll be there?"

"Swear."

"Something did come for you today."

Here we go again.

"Not another article from Cousin Isaac?" I'm scared. "Look, that's his heritage. It's part of his DNA. I'm more flexible, genetically speaking."

"Who's Sydney?"

"My heroine on *Melrose Place.* The one you agreed to free me from any matrimonial obligations if she gave me a second look. Even through the television."

"Well, she's finally replying to all your fan mail."

Deb reveals a beautifully scripted letter. Not from Melrose Sydney, but from bachelor party Sonoma Sydney.

"Oh." Big oh. "Just someone I met in Tahoe."

Through the anger in Deb's green eyes, I see a perfect setup for a horror film: *I Know What You Did at Your Bachelor Party*. The sequel, *I Still Remember What You Did at Your Bachelor Party and Will Never Forget It, So Don't Try and Change the Subject,* surely isn't far behind.

Why did I give Sydney my address? Damn free casino drinks. Why did Deb open my mail? Damn power of attorney. At least I gave Sydney my cell number, not our home number. Not that it mattered. We only talked once. She still was in need of great sex. And I still wasn't the guy for the job. I've spoken with a few of my ex-girlfriends recently. Some by chance, some by choice. Either way, the conversations weren't as fulfilling as I envisioned. No one begged me to reconsider, let alone put on the French maid outfit I innocently suggested during our third month of dating.

"Mind explaining this?" Deb asks with no more than a millimeter between us.

So much for our don't-ask, don't-tell approach to the bachelor party. Now I am being presented with physical evidence of the festivities, bank withdrawals notwithstanding. What would I do if that were a letter for Deb from a guy eager to give her money while they both drank lots of alcohol? Demand answers, that's what. Should I maintain a double standard? Walk out and say it's none of her business?

I reveal some, not all.

"That's it?" Deb wonders.

"Yeah. Nothing much. Just a wacky rich girl at the casino. She really hung around the others. I was too busy gambling our way into a nest egg." I laugh my way to the couch. Not a laugh like when you see a dozen fat clowns exit a Yugo. More like a laugh when you see that same fat clown-filled Yugo crushed by a pissed-off circus elephant.

Then Deb pulls out the pictures. Why do there always have to be pictures?

"Anything else you want to tell me?" she snorts.

Did I prematurely confess? Did I mysteriously forget a couple hours of very bad behavior that mysteriously showed up on film? How bad could these Kodak moments be? Bravely, I look. The heiress and I sitting at the blackjack table, sharing an over-sized tropical drink. The heiress kissing me on the cheek. Me kissing the heiress, also on the cheek. The two of us wrestling outside the casino. Nothing too terrible.

Then Deb reads the letter out loud. How thoughtful of the heiress to wish us luck with the wedding. But she didn't have to end it with "Ha Ha" and remind me about that "great screw I promised" her.

"What does that mean? What did you tell her? What did you do with her? You really are ruining this marriage. Do you know that?"

"Look, sweetie. I can dance. I can dance."

I glide around the room, showing off all the moves we learned last night. But my twirling fails to win Deb's love back. Or even cause a sufficient distraction. The two-stepping stops, and the back-stepping resumes.

"Was she serious?" Deb questions.

"The only thing her royal heiress of Sonoma reigned over was a state of drunkenness. She professed her desires to all who walked by."

"Swear?"

"Swear."

"You still want to get married?"

"Can't wait."

"Did you sleep with any hookers?"

Replying with a prolonged "What?" would have been too much of a tip-off to my other innocent misadventures. Fortunately, I had enough composure to answer this one properly. "Of course not!"

Deb accepts this at face value. I get off easy. It's great that no matter how many weird notes come in the mail from strange women, Deb is going to trust me. I just got mail from someone I met on my bachelor party talking about sex with photos of us kissing. And Deb's taking it in stride. I wonder if she would be acting different if the heiress was Jewish? Would she think that was a secret mission sanctioned by Cousin Isaac? Would that make her Latin blood boil over? Which would then make my Jewish blood spill over.

✧

PIZZA IS SERVED once again. This time over Scrabble, something Deb and I haven't played for a while. Of course, to cool tensions, I'll let Deb win. She usually does anyway.

Inside the Scrabble box we keep previous scores and some of the fun words played. I compare our second date with our current board tiles.

Second date words	Today's words
SMOOCH	BANKRUPT
ROMANCE	LAWYER
DESIRE	SLEEP
BABYOIL	ASPIRIN
TICKLES	SPACE

Deb wins with KNOT (how fitting), and wedding-ring tensions lower a few notches.

During my hard day at work, I bought a web domain for Deb. "Call it an early wedding present."

"Oh joy. What is it?"

"TeamMichaels.com. Isn't that cool?"

"You never cease to amaze me."

"Thanks. See, I'm serious about a family. First there was CraigMichaels.com. Then came CraigAndDeb.com, which is all about us. Now I am preparing for expansion. Hence TeamMichaels.com."

"Forgive my lack of excitement."

"I even thought of a slogan. Fun, but frugal."

Deb's really excited now. More like agitated. Why did I open my mouth? Why couldn't I have just used that gap in my head to cram in another slice of pizza?

"You're fully turning cheap on me, aren't you?"

"No. We just need to have a better spending plan than what we're used to."

"What does that mean?"

"Didn't you hear 'fun?' It's not like I said 'frugal and sad.' Or just frugal. Fun is good, right? Don't cry."

Must be pre-wedding jitters. It can't all be my fault.

Can it?

SURVEY SAYS:
GET READY FOR A FAMILY FEUD

HAIRS WILL RISE. Worlds will collide. Fists may fly. But what else would you expect when dealing with family. Hers and yours.

The In-Laws

Remember, she's their daughter. You might have been sleeping with her for the past few years, but they've tucked her in long before your slimy hands fouled their precious princess. Here are a few ways to make your entry into their world more pleasant:

- **Be patient.** It's a trying time for everyone. Especially for those paying for your premium shelf alcohol, twenty-piece band, and mountaintop wedding for five hundred. Understand their perspective.
- **Be supportive.** Show that you love their daughter. Nothing offers a greater return than their feeling that their daughter made a good decision. Give in on the little wedding issues (at least what should be little decisions in your mind), like flower colors, dress colors, and anything colors. It's not worth the fight. Plus, you look like the accommodating one. Which is much sexier than six-pack abs at this moment.
- **Be involved.** Help with the planning. Act interested in their lives. Spend time with them. Don't just answer their questions. Engage in actual conversation. You might want to avoid discussing politics, abortion rights, religion, and the time you partied all night at the Playboy Mansion. Unless your fiancée was Miss November.

- **Be diplomatic.** Watch out for family arguments. You might be forced to take sides. Sometimes you may want to go against your fiancée in a decision. Tread carefully. While you might score points with your future father-in-law, you might get thrown out of the game by your fiancée.
- **Be aware.** You might not want to be a big part of their family, and they might not want you, either. Lucked out? Hopefully. Just watch out for families who want to smother their daughter but freeze you out. After all, the old saying is true. You're not just marrying her, but her family.

Your Family

- Remember, your mom and dad have opinions, too. Which should count for something, especially if they didn't spank you too much growing up, gave you a car for a graduation present, and may continue paying your allowance even after the wedding.
- Make your family want to like your fiancée. Hopefully, they've met her before you proposed. But what's done is done. Bring her home every now and then. Ask your fiancée to keep an open mind as your mom expresses her thoughts on the wedding. These thoughts may range from the totally acceptable to the totally off-the-wall, depending on whether you have sisters, your parents have been to a wedding this decade, and you visit home more than once a year.
- Be a good son, but keep in mind you're about to be someone's husband. The time to hide behind your mom's apron is long gone. Your fiancée expects to see someone who can handle himself, make decisions, and protect his future family.
- It's nice to give your family some wedding tasks to perform. They don't have to be elaborate. Just make them

feel wanted and appreciated. As you have probably already figured out, there are more than enough tasks to go around. If you haven't figured this out by now, you might want to re-read every page of this book.

- It might be a good idea to discuss with your fiancée how you're going to handle holiday visits, especially if your families live in different cities. You're probably used to it by now, but it only gets worse. Think kids. Think airplanes. Think kids on airplanes. If you can afford it, buy a big house. Big enough to host holidays.

- Try to get your families together before the wedding. It doesn't have to be long, heart-wrenching visits, but you want them to be somewhat friendly for the guests, officiant, and videographer. A neutral, non-wedding-related meeting ground, like a restaurant, park, or musical, might help bridge the families. Or at least avoid a massacre.

HONK IF YOU'RE
GETTING HITCHED.

I was married by a judge.
I should have asked for a jury.
(George Burns)

"THE VEGAS EXPRESS leaves in thirty minutes," I yell out. Deb and her family are making the nine-hour trek in a rental van.

"Last chance. I know you want to hop in," Deb offers.

"I'll stick with my flight tomorrow. Looks like it would be a tight squeeze."

This isn't your standard rental van I'm loading up. It's a mini-wedding on wheels. I cram in the wedding dress (triple-boxed to keep my prying eyes away), a seamstress tool set capable of outfitting an army, a first-aid kit worthy of an Everest climb, and enough makeup to cover every Rockette at Radio City Music Hall. I think the fifty-dollar backup dress is being driven under separate cover. It, too, getting greater protective service than the president.

Could this van be the start of a new business?

Lose a nail?
Missing some lace?
Forget an usher?
Dial 1-800-WED-HELP

I tap the back of the van after I finally slam the doors shut. I feel like a paramedic who just loaded a critical patient in the ambulance, sending her off to life-saving surgery.

I'll miss Deb. But not enough to brave riding the "I Do or Bust" bus.

The van heads off into the horizon. I wave until I can't see it anymore. Then I wave an extra ten minutes. Just in case something is forgotten and Deb heads back. Or she decides to test my love.

NOT MANY VAN updates from Interstate Five. The few calls I get are brief, but reveal much.

"The drive is too long."
"Deb's a bit moody."
"Deb's a bit queasy."
"We're on another bathroom break. This will be your job
    soon, son."
"Deb is in no mood to speak."

Way too many emotions must be flying around. Every last detail, especially all the ones that I did not help with, will be painstakingly scrutinized. My "go with the flow" attitude wouldn't help my cause. Or protect me from bodily harm. It's better to breathe the fresh air of bachelorhood far away from the van for a few hours longer.

Deb does call around hour six of the "From Living in Sin to Wedding in Sin City" tour.

"Are you still sure about getting married?" she inquires.

"I think so."

No response for what feels like an eternity.

Then I hear the blare of horns in the background. Bawling in the foreground. Out of all the answers I could have given, did I choose the one that drives the van off the freeway? I must have set Deb back a few hours of deep meditation.

"We gotta go," Deb's mom says.

Click.

✦

RADIO SILENCE FOR the rest of the day. Did I really set Deb off the deep end? Am I ready to take the plunge? What about my ten-year plan? Will marriage get in the way of my first Oscar? What about my third? Will I ever make it on Letterman? I don't think a wedding will help or hurt that. Some men might feel weighted down with a wife and family, but Deb's done nothing to cause me concern. She has always encouraged me to pursue my dreams. Will getting married change that? Will marriage change her and what she wants? What does she want? Besides me, of course (if I want to make in Hollywood, I've got to have an ego). I can't help but worry if Deb's attitude will change after the wedding. Is this is one of those things I won't know until it's too late? Like buying a car, but without the lemon laws. Or accepting a job, but without the at-will work laws. Yes, there are laws to get out of a marriage. But I've got to have faith.

I leave work early. My last night alone. What to do?

A) Go for a ride in Deb's convertible, letting the ocean breeze run through my hair?
B) Write a love poem to recite at the ceremony?
C) Hit the gym for a final workout to help me fit into my tux?
D) Consume an extra-large pizza and veg with a *Simpsons* marathon while I pack?

Survey says D.

What to pack? Where's Deb when I need her? I feel as clueless as when I packed for our fifth date/ten-day trip to Costa Rica. I feel the same sense of excitement and anticipation for the wedding and honeymoon trip. And once again, I scramble to search for underwear without holes.

✧

DEB AND I knew nothing about each other before jumping on that plane to Costa Rica. Granted we did have a few date-friendly conversations under our belt. We were able to learn about where each of us grew up, confirm each other's phone numbers (was it wrong to put Deb's in an envelope marked "Who to blame if Craig isn't heard from again?"), and get a taste of what foods we each like. Anyone's normal stuff.

Of course, I just had to keep up all of my little fibs sprinkled into my life story. Swiss bank accounts. Weekends in Paris. Marathon training. My normal stuff. At least through the trip. No sense in disappointing Deb until we land back on U.S. soil. Actually, we had been quite honest and open about our interests, goals, and how much I wanted to sleep with her. Well, that last one was purely inner monologue, but I could have sworn she heard the pleas echoing around my head.

At least we kissed before leaving the country. But what else were we going to do for ten days? I assumed we'd progress beyond kissing. And do more than sightseeing. Especially since for all Deb knows I actually do have the body of a marathon runner. I had to be prepared. My night-before extensive research of Central America revealed that beer was cheaper than water (and often safer), so the forces of impaired sexual judgment were on my side. Unfortunately, my research didn't provide much detail on the availability of birth control in the Costa Rican countryside.

Thus I did what any red-blooded man about to embark on a romantic adventure with a red-blooded woman would do. I hightailed it to Costco, bought, and packed an entire case of condoms for the trip. Simple mathematics. Nine days (I discounted the first day for getting acquainted) times three "events" a day. Allow for a few mishandlings. That comes to about a case. Or a quart if you do the liquid conversion.

OUR COSTA RICAN adventure went exceedingly well. With one exception. A resort we stayed at was originally only planned for Deb. While the accommodations were ample enough for two, the bathroom had what can only be called an interesting design detail: no door. The toilet wasn't in the middle of the room; it was off to the side. However, there were no visual; audio; and, most important, olfactory barriers to assist in keeping at least some things a surprise in the relationship. So, instead of using the spacious marble built-in accommodations (which were bigger than most rooms in our current apartment), whenever nature called, we had to leave our villa for the public bathrooms meant for the campsite next to the resort.

Yes, we did have sex. No, it wasn't three times a day, but one had to plan for the worst (or best). And besides the romance, there were many other great discoveries and bonds made on that trip. Enough for me to know that Deb was the one for me. And I hoped enough for Deb to reach that same conclusion. Fortunately, I didn't reveal all of my feelings to Deb as soon as we got back (I'm not *that* Mr. Uncool). But a sufficient amount was mutually shared in the weeks after our trip to set our relationship on a high-speed path toward love; proposal; engagement; and, in about three days, marriage.

I'm sure our honeymoon will in many ways resemble our trip to Costa Rica. Although I did double-verify that all bathrooms had doors and locks (we're still not that open in our relationship). But what about our marriage? Will it be full of just ups, like Costa Rica? How many downs, like wedding planning, should I expect? And how many is too many? Being alone today makes me question if I lived enough on my own to know when it's the right time to start sharing a place (and not just cohabitate)?

Was I right in saying that true wedding panic won't kick in until the last two hundred and fifty thousand seconds? Because that's what our Web site countdown says. And I'm panicking.

Maybe I should have taken my chances in the van.

Or at least ordered an extra-extra-large pizza.

HEED THE BOY SCOUTS WARNING: BE PREPARED

HERE'S A HANDY emergency kit for you to pack to ensure smooth sailing on your wedding day.

For you and her, just in case

Antacid	Aspirin
Band-aids	Black socks
Bottle of water	Breath mint
Comb	Credit card
Deodorant	Directions to ceremony and reception
Extra set of keys (car and house)	Glue
Matches	Numbers of wedding party and vendors
PowerBar	Prescription medication
Sewing kit and safety pins	Spare change
Tissues	Toothbrush and toothpaste
Wedding license	

For you, just in case

Mini vodka bottles (can also clean wounds)	Novelty wedding rings
Condoms	Duct tape
Mind-altering medication	Names of fiancée family members
One hundred dollars in small bills	Second passport
Alternative identities	Spare underwear
Untraceable cell phone	
Translating dictionary for a country that doesn't have an extradition treaty with United States	

YOU'RE TOAST

THERE ARE TWO key occasions where you're expected to say thanks: the rehearsal dinner and the reception. Of course, if you love an audience, you'll probably be begging for more speaking engagements. But in terms of your wedding, you need to focus.

Rehearsal dinner toast

A barest-of-bare-bones rehearsal dinner toast consists of:

- Thanking your fiancée for picking you.
- Thanking your parents for this event and for being there for all these years.
- Thanking your groomsmen for their support (or lack thereof).
- Thanking the bridesmaids for their support (or at least fiancée diversions).
- Thanking everyone for coming.
- Feel free to thank others, share a family anecdote, and extend loving praise to your fiancée.

- Do practice.
- Do thank everyone.
- Do express love and appreciation to your family, especially your mom.
- Do give a PG-rated toast.

- Don't give a graphic recount of the bachelor party.
- Don't take too long.
- Don't lament over the one that got away.
- Don't drink too much before your toast. After your toast, it's fair game.

Reception toast

A barest-of-bare-bones reception toast consists of:

- Your appreciation and love of your new wife.
- Your appreciation of your wife's parents for hosting the wedding and sharing their daughter.
- Your appreciation of your family.
- Your appreciation of the bridal party.
- Your appreciation of your guests for joining in the festivities.
- A sappy comment on your commitment and devotion to your wife and your new life together.
- A toast to your wife.
- Kissing your wife.

Here's what you should say:

I want to thank everyone for traveling far and wide to be here today.

(*Fiancée's name*), you are the one and only for me. I knew this from the moment we met (*Number of years you've known fiancée*) years ago. Thank you for picking me.

To (*Fiancée's name*)'s family, I appreciate all that you have done to make this day so special, including raising such a (*Adjective describing your fiancée*) woman. Not only am I blessed to be starting a new life with (*Fiancée's name*), but I am so happy that I can share our great moments with you as well.

Now, as far as my family goes. Who would have known that your boy who (*Favorite childhood moment shared with parents*) would be here today? I owe a great deal to you. Thanks for all of your support and understanding through the years.

There are so many people to thank; I can go on for hours. But I'll be brief. After all, we still have more partying to do. To our wedding party, you've been a part of our lives either separately or as a couple, or both. We've had great times, and you've helped up through not-so-great times. I can only hope that our bonds will grow even stronger. And (*Best man's name*), I will never forget (*Favorite moment shared with best man*). After that, who else could I choose to be my best man?

Okay, enough with the thanks. (*Fiancée's name*), you are my best friend and partner for life . . . and I couldn't be happier. I love you.

To (*Fiancée's name*)!

Here's what you probably want to say:

I want to thank everyone for sharing this day with us. But most important, I want to thank my (*Adjective describing your fiancée*) bride, (*Fiancée's name*). How did I get so lucky? I love you with all my heart. And it shows given how (*choose one: very helpful / somewhat helpful / not helpful*) I was with the planning. I figured that was the best course of action.

To (*Fiancée's name*)'s family, many thanks for raising such a wonderful woman. And for letting me sleep with her before committing. I don't know whose sex genes she has, but I do know I can't wait to get her out of her jeans every chance I get.

To my family, many thanks for putting up with me, especially during (*Favorite childhood moment shared with parents*). I wouldn't be the person I am today without that special moment.

To (*Best man's name*), my best man, remember when we (*Favorite moment shared with best man*)? Go figure I still wanted to get married.

Now, will everyone please raise their glass and join me in a toast?

(*Depending on how involved you were in deciding to get married*)

You wanted it: I can't wait to begin the rest of my life with you. I love you.

You agreed to it: You are my best friend and partner. Here's to us.

You were forced into it: Guess we should have better separated your birth control from the Tic Tacs.

To (*Fiancée's name*)!

5

NOW I'M READY TO DO MY PART. WHAT IS IT AGAIN?

Three days to go

Attend rehearsal and dinner

Practice makes perfect. Hence the rehearsal. Make sure your fiancée is happy. Now's the time to make any changes (other than changing fiancées).

The best man and host (usually your father) should make toasts at the dinner. You and your fiancée should thank the wedding party and your parents as well. Also, now is the time to hand out your groomsmen gifts.

Have a big breakfast

Don't be the malnourished groom that passes out from the stress. Be the well-fed groom who can hold his liquor all night.

Get luggage ready

If you're not packed by now, prepare to increase your credit card limits for all that honeymoon hotel lobby shopping you'll be doing.

Give ring to best man

Check for pocket holes first. Don't dig too deep and give any-one doubts on why you are marrying a woman.

Bring marriage license

Ignorance isn't a valid excuse at this point.

Turn off cell phone

If the caller is that important, don't you think you should have invited him or her to the wedding?

Don't be late

Even in movies, this move can be fatal.

Say "I do"

And after you affirm your intentions, take a deep breath and enjoy the moment. The best is about to come.

Socialize at wedding

Your guests traveled far and wide to join you today. And even if they didn't, you should still thank everyone for sharing in your special day. Don't just hang with your bride. You'll have the next four or five decades for that. Mingle. Dance with guests. Smile for pictures. Also, eat some food. Most couples forget to enjoy what they spent all their money on.

Speak up

The first few toasts will be about you (from the best man, maid of honor, and your bride's father). Then it's your turn to speak. This is your chance to toast your new bride, thank your families (especially your in-laws), and thank friends for coming.

Seal the deal

Don't go to sleep without officially sanctioning the wedding. And satisfying your new wife. But, if you only get one out of two done, at least you're married. Where else can she go?

OLD TO-DO'S LEFT TO DO

How late am I?

Shop for honeymoon clothes	2 months
Pick up wedding rings	2 months
Pour your heart out (write vows, speeches, and toasts)	2 weeks
Pick up license	1 week
Pick up tuxedo	1 week

PRACTICE
MAKES PERFECT.

A successful marriage requires falling in love many times,
always with the same person.
(Mignon McLaughlin)

"MISS ME?" DEB asks from the Four Seasons in Las Vegas. Her voice suggests a bit more confidence than during the van ride.

"Miss you," I respond, still packing.

"Three days."

"Technically, really two. One if you discount travel. But who's counting?"

"It's going to be a long life if you start counting now. Did you get your ring?"

"Already packed."

"Promise?"

"Promise."

"Promise?" I ask Ted, a coworker in the kitchen at work.

"Promise," Ted replies. "You can use mine if yours doesn't arrive today."

Ring contingency plan secured. Being model size ten pays off yet again.

Nico stares at me the whole morning.

"Do you realize you'll be married the next time you come back here?" Nico ponders.

"I'll still be me."

"Right, mate. Me. Don't you mean me and the missus? There's a good pick-up line."

Brushing Nico's comments aside, I tell myself to enjoy married life. But is married life a contradiction? A conundrum? No time to dwell. There'll be plenty of time for contemplation over the years (and years and years) to come.

My ring arrives. Thank you, God. And thank you, Ted, for the almost-use of his ring during the next two weeks. I rip open the package, just to make sure cheapplatinum.com didn't take any liberties with my order. Liberties that might severely limit my liberties once Deb found out I lied about already packing my ring.

The band slips on nicely, but my body feels off balance. My left side is now heavier than the right. I can't lift my left arm above my waist. Is there some truth to the relationship enigma that man has pondered for centuries? How can something so small weigh so much?

I TRY TO leave work quietly, but am stopped at the atrium by a pack of coworkers, ready to give me the obligatory send-off cheer.

From the men	From the women
"You still have time to run."	"This will be the best weekend."
"Don't do anything I wouldn't do. Besides marry."	"Cherish Deb."
"Glad it's not me."	"You're so lucky."
"Remember, ten bucks on black."	"Savor every moment."
"My gift is in the mail."	"Wish it were me."

Wish it were me? What does that mean? Should I take that literally? Who said that?

I make it to the airport on time. Board my flight without a hitch. Don't share a word with anyone. This is it. The next ground I touch will be the landmass that will change my life forever. Unconsciously, I grip my seatmate's arm. Just as Deb grips mine whenever we are on a plane together. I miss Deb. I miss taking care of her. I miss her defending me in times when I do something stupid. Like digging my fingernails into the guy in seat 18B.

"Please, sir, don't press the Call button," I plead.

Besides my pre-takeoff groping with 18B, the flight is an uneventful start to an eventful weekend. Deb and I are keeping separate quarters until wedding night. "Tradition," she said. Deb has a suite in the Four Seasons. I have the cheapest room available in the Mandalay Bay. We're actually in the same building, but while she gets unlimited spa services, better food, and lots of pampering, I get to drink tap water for my two hundred dollars a night. Fun, but frugal.

DEB'S NOWHERE IN sight. Probably being wrapped in seaweed to brighten her complexion. I lunch with Jenny, Deb's oldest friend and maid of honor. She does a great job of calming my nerves with some childhood stories of Deb, including the time she almost burned down her house.

Suddenly my hair stands up. I shudder. Nothing to do with Jenny's most recent wild, single-Deb story ("Deb didn't really date the whole football team? Did she?"). I sense that my family has just landed.

We head over to the rehearsal. The differences between the wedding parties surface again during our rehearsal. The women act like Army Special Forces, protecting and anticipating Deb's every need.

"More champagne?"
"Sit. I'll take care of it."
"Of course he means well."

The men act like Hogan's Heroes, leaving me and escaping to the safety of the nearest craps table every chance they get.

"You don't need me right now, do you?"

"Can I borrow a twenty?"

"Odds on the six."

Everyone's blown away by the resort's beauty. The sky is blue. The lake and hills are picture perfect. The temperature is just right. As such, the Vegas cheese factor diminishes. Then an errant golf ball hits me in the leg. Two guys in plaid pants and Hawaiian shirts drive up to play through. Well, a little cheese might not be so bad.

We line up. We walk. We stand. We listen as Reverend Julie takes us through the ceremony highlights.

Deb and I hold hands. Tight, but not too tight. Our eyes lock every few seconds.

"This is great," I whisper.

Deb smiles.

"You're great," I add.

Deb hugs me.

"We're great," I conclude.

"I'm great. You're just along for the ride," Deb jabs. Then she kisses me.

" . . . then I'll announce you as man and wife," Reverend Julie finishes.

I think I caught all the steps. I better re-read the program tonight just to be sure.

Afterward, Deb and I check up on the flowers, chairs, food, staff, and schedule. Well, Deb checks up. I just continue to hold her hand. At some point, she'll give it a squeeze. That's my cue to curse at the planner for forgetting the correct chair covers.

✧

OUR FAMILIES COMFORTABLY mingle at the rehearsal dinner. All it takes is my mom and Deb's mom swapping potty training stories. Fortunately, Drew breaks up this dirty diaper-filled moment with a few words.

"Craig was so happy when Deb said those three magical words. 'That's him, officer.'"

Now he decides to roast me.

Fortunately, my dad comes to the rescue and welcomes Deb and her family to our family.

"I hope you checked your sanity at the door," Dad says.

After dinner, Deb goes off with her family to bond. I'm off with my family to bond as well: blackjack with Uncle Bob.

"Feeling lucky?" Scott, our dealer from Cleveland, asks.

"I'm getting married in two days," I reply as Scott goes around the table. "You tell me."

"Dealer gets blackjack," Scott announces.

So much for surprising Deb with a necklace from the hotel's overpriced jewelry store. Or a bracelet. Or a toe ring. After Scott cleans me out I have just enough left to buy Deb a gold-sparkled Vegas hair scrunchie at the gift shop. It's on sale next to the laminated "Win at Blackjack" betting card I should have purchased before walking into the casino.

"Must be lucky in love," Scott offers as I pocket twenty dollars in chips—what's left of the three hundred I started with.

Bob's doing better. He tosses me a hundred-dollar chip. "Extra wedding present. But give the money to Deb, not the casino. Go to bed."

✧

IT'S 3 AM. I'm back in my hotel room. What's Deb doing? Sleeping? Partying? Gambling? She can't be out later than me. If she is, maybe I should be the one wearing the three-thousand-dollar dress. Actually, I'd be the one wearing the fifty-dollar dress and putting the two thousand nine hundred and fifty dollars in our future children's therapy fund.

I need contact. Room-to-room call? Too desperate. And might wake up Deb's bridesmaids, who are no doubt exhausted from helping Deb. Cell call? Ditto. Text message? Why not? It's the proper mix of affection and separation in this technological day and age.

"HOW R U?" I key in.

"NAUSEOUS," she replies. "U?"

"POORER. NOT 2 MANY 21s."

"IT'S OK. LESS MONEY = MORE TIME 4 LOVE :-)"

I am definitely marrying the right person.

PLAYING THE WEDDING-HORROR BINGO GAME

WHAT CAN GO wrong at the wedding? A lot.

Of course, your wedding will go as smooth as glass. Fingers crossed. Wood knocked. Minister tipped (and not tipsy).

However, you might want to hand out game cards for your friends just in case things get a bit bumpy. No need for everyone to have a bad time while your wedding is ruined, bride is crying, and in-laws are choking you.

Your friends should check off each block if they witness an event in the game card. The first person to observe five blocks horizontally, vertically, or diagonally should stand up and shout "Bingo!" You might be too busy fighting the fires that caused the bingo to award any prizes, but that won't stop your friends from enjoying the party.

B	I	N	G	O
Bride/Groom runs away	Guest gets food poisoning	Bride is pregnant	Wrong name said during vows	Curses in toast
Nudity during slide show (non-baby)	Someone objects	Bride/Groom is late	Bride's dress rips	Mystery meat is main course
Gifts get stolen	Mom-in-law can't stop crying	**FREE SPACE**	Cops break up fight	Conga line
Rains during outdoor reception	Groom forgets ring	Riot during bouquet toss	Premium beer = Coors	Bride/Groom Ex makes scene
Plastic silverware	Bride dirty dances (non-Groom)	Eye poked during garter toss	Drunk relative makes scene	CPR administered

STANDING ROOM ONLY

AT THE ALTAR, the groom traditionally stands on the bride's right side. In olden days, Mr. Groom would have held Ms. Bride with his left hand and wielded a sword with his right just in case Ms. Bride had a Mr. Man On The Side who wanted to put a stop to the union.

The receiving line is where the newlyweds greet their guests. It was once believed that touching the bride and groom would bring guests good luck because, on their wedding day, the couple was blessed by the gods. Now it's more about being reminded who the heck Aunt Carol is. Don't worry, your bride will whisper it in your ear.

LICENSE
TO WED.

When a woman gets married
it's like jumping into a hole in the ice in the middle of winter.
You do it once, and you remember it the rest of your days.
(Maxim Gorky)

LOTS LEFT TO do, but at least the rehearsal taught me how to survive the ceremony. Lead with my right foot, stand straight, and don't stare at the crowd too long. Also, try not to dart my eyes around. And, heaven forbid, don't roll them at any point. No need to ruin the wedding DVD with any poorly timed close-ups.

The men need to pick up our tuxedos. Seven of us pile into the minivan, which is much roomier without the bridal survival kit. I cannot blame Deb for staying clear of this excursion. She might lose it as I try to cat herd the men around Vegas.

Actually, I feel more like Noah, transporting animals of all shapes and sizes to safety. Well, at least to wardrobe. I have them all. Tall. Short. Old. Young. Skinny. Barrel-shaped. Everyone's spirits are high but mine. My spirits seem to be trapped in stomach knots.

With the exception of one last-minute, larger-pant-size scramble ("Patrick, lay off the buffets!"), we're able to leave

Mr. Tux with seven pants, vests, ties, shirts, and jackets; fourteen cufflinks and shoes; and twenty-eight button studs. I should know. I double-counted them all three times before closing the minivan door. Deb would be proud.

✧

I LUNCH WITH my family poolside at the hotel. Another perfect eighty-degree day. Not a cloud in the sky.

"Guess that rain insurance paid off," I joke.

"You bought rain insurance?" Dad asks.

"Of course," I respond. Obviously, it's tough trying to convince the table that I honestly believe buying rain insurance in sunny Las Vegas was the most logical and reasonable course of action. Tough on its own, but even tougher with a brother attending Yale Law.

Fortunately, Jon is too busy with pen and paper to object. He's working on his toast. Draft number fourteen by his latest count.

Lunch turns out well. Granted, I cannot eat solids, but Dad slips me a thousand dollars in "honeymoon and beyond" spending money. Should I double-down on our rain insurance? After all, I'm getting one-hundred-to-one odds.

✧

WE HOST A western hoe-down at Gilley's, a country bar in the Frontier hotel. Since everyone's from out of town, we want to have something to bring the guests together before the big day. Gilley's offers barbeque, square-dancing, and bull-riding. Can anything be more fitting? A lot of things, according to Deb. But Gilley's was the most reasonably priced place. Fun, but frugal. I imagine Deb will inscribe this on my headstone. I hope I at least get to enjoy the honeymoon before she puts me out of her misery.

I arrive early in bolo tie, Wrangler jeans, and a Texas-shaped belt buckle. Deb's stranded at a nail salon ten miles away. I am not sure why, with all the expenses being incurred, she decided to head off-Strip to get her nails done. My frugality influence?

"No, cowboy. There weren't any places close by that had an appointment," Deb barely suppresses a scream.

"Do you want me to pick you up?"

"Just stay there and mingle. A cab will be here soon."

I run out of ice-breaking, keep-guests-entertained, sidestep-the-where's-Deb-question material within five minutes.

"Who's from out of town?"

"Glad you could make it."

"Who are you? A new cousin? Great."

"I'm six-foot-five. Nope, never played basketball."

"Try the Buckeye Burger, I hear it is delicious."

I'm pleased to see all my groomsmen have made it on time and relatively appropriately dressed. Of course, they aren't trying to work the room like I am. But then again, they're not the groom.

After another hour and a dozen sob-filled phone updates, Deb arrives. Her nails look great. Only a few tear stains mar the rich beige gloss.

"Don't say it," Deb pleads.

All my groomsmen ride the mechanical bull. As I start to hop on Ol' Bessie, I get The Stare. The same one I got after I contemplated getting an ear pierced in high school. "Do you want to walk into a boardroom one day with a hole in your head?" Mom asked. Like then, I graciously decline the pain-inflicting offer, which is actually a good thing. While I probably could handle a boardroom presentation with a piercing, I would hate to hobble down the aisle tomorrow with a pin in my hip. Even if the bull operator promises to lower the setting to Cowpoke.

I settle for the group line-dancing lesson. Mom's happy. Deb's happy. Deb's mom's happy. My male ego? It's survived worse.

Deb and I leave the party early to pick up our marriage license. Nothing like waiting until the last minute. Deb's beyond nervous. She sticks her head out the window in front of Circus Circus, only one block into our journey. She cannot control her nervous heaving. I begin to heave as well. Not sympathetic heaves. Not nerves. More because I'm cruising the Strip in a minivan. After all, I have a reputation to keep up. Wait, my rep's in Reno. I'm still cool. Line-dancing aside.

"Why don't we hit a drive-thru chapel and get the wedding out of the way?" I offer.

"Can't . . ." Deb moans.

"We won't tell anyone. And we'll still get married tomorrow."

"Can't . . ."

"Why not?"

"Can't keep it in."

There goes Deb's dinner.

"We should have eloped," Deb admits in between gut-wrenches.

Time to be the compassionate and loving mate. "I told you so!" I couldn't resist. But I say it in the most loving way possible, holding her head up to keep the vomit off her nails. And my cowboy boots.

We pull into the nearest convenience store, and I force Deb to drink a two-liter of ginger ale. Now that's compassion.

The Clark County Clerk Office is open until midnight during the week and never closes on weekends. It's now twelve-thirty on Saturday morning. The wedding is less than fourteen hours away. There are four groups waiting in line for a marriage license:

Couple. Old. In tux and gown.
Couple. Our age. In tux and gown. Bride's seven months
     pregnant. God bless Lycra.
Me. Deb's in the bathroom. Again.
Couple. Young. In casual attire. Mother of bride in tow.

A clerk approaches the line. Is he going to hand out door prizes to the best dressed? The worst dressed? The pathetic guy by himself?

"Glad you came back," he tells the young couple behind me. "I checked. You do have to be sixteen to get married. Unless you go in front of a judge."

At least there's some sensibility in Vegas.

"When can we do that?" the mother asks.

So much for sensibility.

Deb's back from the bathroom. A few shades paler, but her nails still look good. Well, they look a mess, but I won't be the one to tell her that.

We step up to the counter to fill out our application. Since we are handed golf pencils to write with and the form is only five inches long, application is an overstatement. Just enough room for our name, address, social security number, and the number of previous marriages. Slowly we each write zero, watching to make sure that's what the other is doing. No divorce skeletons. Good. No more food inside Deb's stomach. Better.

Fifteen minutes later, license secured. On with the wedding!

But first, out with the ginger ale. Not a pretty sight in the parking lot behind the minivan. I drop Deb off at the Four Seasons and give her one last pre-husband-and-wife kiss. It's not too hot and heavy. I know what has passed through her lips this evening.

No use trying to sleep. I meet Cousin Isaac at the Hard Rock Casino. He's bunking with me tonight to not only lower the cost of the room, but hopefully my fear level as well. That's what he says, but I'm prepare for one last "are you sure you want to stray from the flock?" sermon.

Another four hundred dollars of mine gets deposited to the Bank of Las Vegas. I've had enough. Isaac is just getting started (fortunately, the glitter of Vegas makes him forget his lecture). I give him a goodnight kiss, bigger than Deb's. To let the world (or at least the women close by) know how much I love him. I'm in no mood for him to bring a date back to our hotel room tonight.

LET THEM EAT CAKE!

THE WEDDING CAKE symbolizes fertility. Ancient Romans used to break a thin layer of cake over the bride's head at the end of the ceremony to ensure her fertility. Guests would take the crumbs as good luck tokens. In medieval England, guests would pile small cakes together for the bride and groom to kiss over them. At some point, a French baker decided to ice all the cakes together into a large one, which is what we have today.

Cutting the cake represents the start of the bride and groom's life together. The groom places his right hand over the bride's to guide it for the first cut. Superstition requires that the bride cut the first piece. The groom feeds the bride first, and then she feeds him, symbolizing their first meal together.

Be sure to curb your sweet tooth. You would gain about thirteen pounds if you decide to eat the entire cake.

Source: "A Nice Ring to It," *Men's Health,* June 2002

■

PIMP YOUR RIDE

YOUR WEDDING DAY is no time for you to be behind the wheel. Hire a driver. Rent a fleet. Make an entrance.

There's an abundance of choices when it comes to transportation. Big limos. Small ones. SUVs. Monster trucks. Trolleys. Even horse-drawn carriages. Regardless of what you pick, be sure to stock them with food and drinks for after the ceremony. That's a great time to toast your bride and friends for sharing the day with you. Plus, you never know when you'll be eating next, regardless of the hundreds of pounds of shrimp on ice, chilling for the cocktail hour. If you are going to drink after the ceremony, remember two things: you should be respectful of the ceremony site (some churches may frown on beer bongs on the front lawn) and be mindful that you're probably about to take some pictures (pictures that will sit on your coffee table for years to come).

How you share the ride depends on your budget, wedding party size, and wedding locations. You may opt for having a bride-and-groom-only limo, one big wedding party limo, or a guy limo and girl limo (you should always ride in the girl limo). It's also nice to have a limo or two for your parents and other very close relatives.

What about your guests? Depending on the location, you may want to book shuttle buses to take your guests from hotels to wedding to ceremony and back home again. That way, everyone should be on time and no one will blame you for expensive speeding tickets or suspended licenses.

Make sure you have the cell phone numbers of your drivers and limo company, in case of unforeseen flats, locked keys, or a bad sense of direction. Also, it's a good idea to meet the drivers and inspect the cars before the big day. You don't want any surprises, like a driver with less than stellar hygiene or a pastel-colored Lincoln.

■

LAST-NIGHT REMINDERS FOR NERVOUS GROOMS-TO-BE

- ❦ Shine your shoes.
- ❦ Double-check that you have all tuxedo pieces.
- ❦ Walk around in tuxedo shoes (especially if they aren't yours) and even if it's just you, the shoes, your boxers, a pizza, and the remote control.
- ❦ Put honeymoon bags and travel documents in place where you'll trip over before forgetting.
- ❦ Finish (or start) toast and place notes in jacket pocket.
- ❦ Tie wedding rings to your wrist (if best man doesn't have them already).
- ❦ Take out at least two hundred dollars from ATM (you never know who you'll have to tip).
- ❦ Charge phone.
- ❦ Give yourself a pep talk worthy of Knute Rockne.
- ❦ Avoid any "new" foods (not the night to experiment).
- ❦ Avoid any "old" foods (be mindful of expiration dates in the kitchen).
- ❦ Stop drinking by ten at night.
- ❦ Set alarm one hour earlier than you think you should wake up.
- ❦ Tame any stray nose, ear, and eyebrow hair.
- ❦ Behave well within the bounds of the law.
- ❦ Stay at least one hundred yards away from fiancée.
- ❦ Self-clean your pipes (once is enough—you don't want to injure anything for game day).

I DO.

NOW HIT ME.

*My most brilliant achievement was my ability to
persuade my wife to marry me.
(Winston Churchill)*

FOUR IN THE morning. I'm still alone in my room. Cousin
Isaac's bed is still made up. No use trying to get back to sleep.
If I ever was asleep. I prop myself up in bed, grab a piece of
hotel stationery, and begin writing my wedding speech. I'm
not sure when I'll say it but figure it's better to have this than
stumble on videotape. Like the proposal. Unfortunately, it's
too early and my hand's too shaky to form complete or
coherent sentences. Bullet points will have to do:

Thank friends for coming such a long way. Remind
    everyone it's a dry heat.
Thank family for support. Mention how happy we are for
    new branches on family tree.
Thank Deb for making this happen. And for saying yes.
Pause for "ahhs."
Joke on blowing honeymoon money last night.
Pause for laughs.

Wish everyone well.

Kiss Deb. Easy on tongue.

I go back to sleep, realizing that my last pre-wedding-day to-do is finally a to-done.

✧

"WHAZZUP?" DREW ASKS over the phone. "We're at the buffet. Want to join?"

I lose it. "Can you think of anyone else besides yourself? Now you call me. After you're already there. You know it's MY wedding, right? You're supposed to care about ME."

"Easy. We care. We saved you a seat. Next to the dessert bar."

"Fine." No point arguing. Maybe I just need a good meal.

A meal, not a buffet. Guess I caught Deb's nausea from last night. Granted, I try to buffet. My plate's loaded with standard Vegas fare. Beef. Pasta salad. Cheese omelet. Biscuit and gravy. Macaroni and cheese. But instead of scarfing down the food like everyone else, I wind up in the bathroom with my finger down my throat praying for it all to be over soon. Before this I've been able to keep my nervousness mostly to myself. But now I'm out there for all the strangers in the Luxor's Pharaoh's Pheast Buffet bathroom to see.

My last meal as a single man, and I cannot eat it. I wish my friends would take a moment and worry about me. Or even chew with their mouths closed. I doubt they would stop eating those ribs to hold my head up in the bathroom stall. Maybe if I plan my medical needs around the next turkey delivery at the carving station? Note to self: stop thinking about food.

✧

I HEAD BACK to the hotel. No word from Deb. Not even a text message. She's probably in the middle of a primping storm. At least Cousin Isaac made it back to the hotel room. He's dead to the world.

"Wake up. I have to get ready," I shout.

I could let him sleep in, but my parents are coming over soon to "help me dress." I'd rather not have pictures of Mom picking out my underwear with a man in my bed (even if we're related), so we need to be at least half-dressed before my parents arrive.

"Draw me a bath?" Isaac pleads from under the covers.

How could I refuse? Here I am, trying to resize my tuxedo pants and I have to worry about Isaac's bathwater not being too hot. Thankfully he hasn't called me "Jeeves" yet. In fact, he's polite enough to ask my permission to order room service. Well, he only asked me to call for him, which I gladly do in order to avoid a view of his bubble-covered body stretching from tub to phone.

While on hold ("make sure the eggs aren't runny"), I can't help but stare at Isaac finishing his bath. Have I experienced life from all sides? Nope. Is he the Jewish girl that I was destined for? Very nope.

"For god's sake, cinch that robe," I plead.

While mom and dad help me get dressed (read: clip my bowtie), Isaac (thankfully, also dressed) takes a few pictures. Yes, I am in the middle of a bad Kodak commercial.

"Rendezvous at Loading Zone One. The groomsmen limo is ready," Rick calls to say.

✧

RICK, DREW, JAKE, and Jon are waiting for me. No one knows where Patrick is.

Thirty minutes later, we're still here. Along with most of our guests waiting for their shuttle, who inundate me with too many master-of-the-obvious comments:

"Running late?"
"Still not sure?"
"Did you like the gravy boat we gave you?"
"Shouldn't you be there already?"
"Do I have time to play some craps?"

"For the last time, Jake. No craps!"

Patrick finally arrives. So much for any slack time built into the schedule Deb faxed to my room this morning. I imagine Deb's limo is full of champagne, fresh flowers, and an assortment of fruit and fine cheeses. My limo? It's full of gas-releasing, overstuffed guys lamenting that they forgot to pick up beer. They want to stop, but thanks to Patrick's lateness we can't. Patrick won't explain the delay, but my guess is that he held out for the breakfast-to-lunch shift change at the buffet.

✧

IT'S HOT AT the resort. I'm on pins and needles. But I can see the splendor of everything coming together. I'm sure Deb has had this in her mind since the beginning. I'm impressed. And guilty for not doing more. But the guilt passes as I have to remind Drew not to escort guys to their seats.

Mom and dad are by my side. The Vegas sun is beating down. Yes, I have two sticks of Right Guard caked beneath my ill-fitting tuxedo. And I am staring down the barrel of the aisle. With Reverend Julie in the chamber, locked and ready to fire. My dream is coming alive. But in a good way. A very good way.

My parents say they're glad to be here. And for Deb to join the family. This helps calm my nerves. Until we take our first step. Why must those stomach butterflies be such light sleepers?

I make it to my mark without a trip. I even manage to crack a smile toward the camera.

Then the bridal party approaches the altar. All tuxedo accessories still in order. All bridesmaids looking beautiful in their tangerine halter dresses. Any hint of ruffles or puffiness remain safely sealed in my high school memories.

My brother Jon approaches.

Our nephew Andy with Deb's mom. Andy looks like he would rather be anywhere but here.

Jake and Beth, Deb's cousin. They look good, except for the two-foot height difference. There is one of these mismatches in every wedding party (and prom).

Rick and Annie. I feel bad Annie's married. Not bad for her. Bad for Rick. Most of our guests are married. I hope some of the waitstaff is cute. Not for my sake. For Rick's. I swear. Just for Rick's sake.

Drew and Kim, one of Deb's work friends. Kim was the commander of Deb's special forces. I wish she could have led my troops as well.

Patrick and Christina. Another two-foot difference here. In width, not height.

Jenny, Deb's maid of honor, with each step, goes back and forth between tears and smiles.

All eyes turn to Deb. She looks beautiful. I mouth, "Wow," which I think she sees. Her dress is perfect. It's strapless with shimmering beads, wrapping snugly around her waist and has a bit of a train to it. She's wearing an ivy headpiece with a veil in the back, but not over her face, so we can all see how pretty she looks. My description cannot do justice to the ensemble (I am a guy after all), but Deb puts every bridal magazine cover to shame.

A ray of sun follows her as she walks down with Butch, her godfather. She's beaming. And so am I. We are now standing toe to toe. I wink. She giggles.

As Reverend Julie speaks, I am lucky if I can make out every other word. But I get the gist. Lifelong. Partners. Respect. Love. Trust. Commitment. Endurance. Half romantic expression. Half Tony Robbins power seminar. And it's working—we both feel it.

Every now and then, Deb and I look at each other the same time. We smile. I raise my eyebrows. She nods. We look back at our guests. I am nervous standing here. Not for what's going on. More for how can I get the sweat off my forehead without everyone noticing.

The Hand Blessing goes a bit too long. We hold each other's hands, palms up, while Reverend Julie describes how these hands will cherish, comfort, hold, massage, support, and work for each other. Work? Eyes don't roll. Please don't roll.

And after all the "through this and thats," it's time for the finale.

"I do," Deb professes.

"I do," I proclaim.

We exchange rings.

We break the glass.

We kiss.

People clap.

We're husband and wife.

✧

Do I feel different? Yes and no.

Yes, because the powers vested in the state of Nevada (the same state that allows prostitution, stores nuclear waste, and is home to an airfield of UFOs) have decreed that I'm all Deb's and she's all mine. My heart skips a beat. Then floods my face. I am filled with joy. Then I spring a leak. Tears start coming out. I try to hold back, but it's hard to stop the waterworks.

After all, we have felt so comfortable together; this seems so natural (planning-hell notwithstanding). From our very first encounter, it felt like we were married all along. Now the tears really start to pour out.

Should I take some time to collect my thoughts? Should I try to analyze all the right and wrong in our lives, and develop a family plan? Should I purchase FunButFrugal.com?

Probably. And most likely, I will fret over these things for years to come. But, at this moment, who cares. Let's party!

✧

The reception is only fifty yards from the ceremony site, so it would be hard for anyone to get lost. Everything is outdoors on a circular deck overlooking the lake and surrounded by five-foot-high fireplaces. The table settings look fabulous, incorrect chair covers aside. Note to self: steal a few pieces of silverware as payback and to fill out the registry.

Our families and wedding party get introduced. No trips, stumbles, or falls. Although everyone gasps while Rick performs a rather aggressive dip with Annie during their entrance. I settle for a basic "raise the roof" hand gesture as Deb and I enter the reception. Pretty lame, but at least I didn't do the YMCA like Drew did.

✧

I knew it. Our first dance proves to be a disaster. It was bad enough in the comfort of Serge's San Francisco studio. Who knew how truly awful I'd be with a tux and gown weighing me down? I should have wrapped Deb in a beach umbrella and wore my girdle to prepare for this (versus the jeans and sneakers worn with

Serge). At least Deb's dress hides my shuffling feet. Although I am sure the cameras catch me mouthing more than just sweet nothings on the dance floor.

"SLOW, SLOW, QUICK, QUICK."
"Damn it."
"Sorry."
"Who's leading?"
"Why did you marry me?"

Fortunately, two minutes into the song, the rest of the bridal party joins us. In the camouflage of others, I really begin to put those dance lessons to work. And almost break Deb's toe.

"Through pleasure and pain," I remind Deb.

JON'S TOAST IS spot on. He welcomes Deb as the big sister my mom always wanted. He pokes fun at my penchant for Web sites and suggests I purchase CraigAndDebForever.com. Awws fill the room.

Butch's toast is sweet and sentimental. Especially when he mentions how nice it would have been for Deb's deceased dad Mark to be here. I never had the chance to meet him. I squeeze Deb's hand tight. While we'll always be a part of a larger family (or two), Deb and I are our own family now. Scary, but cool.

IN BETWEEN CONGRATULATORY hugs and kisses, Deb and I do the table walk.

"Well, I did propose," is how I respond to everyone's praise of the event. Deb did an amazing job and I give her all the credit.

Photo ops galore. At the tables. During a spectacular desert sunset. With friends. With strangers (although at a hundred and twenty dollars a plate, these strangers better at least add me to their Christmas card list). Me stealing a bite of cake before it gets wheeled out. During the Chicken Dance. The Conga Line. The Electric Slide. Deb must have slipped that one back in.

I even break-dance a bit. It was really a slow moonwalk away from my doting mother-in-law, but hip-hop is hip-hop.

✧

THE GARTER TOSS is pathetic. My slingshot technique doesn't send it more than two feet. But the really pathetic part is how every guy ran from where it landed. On the other hand, Deb's bouquet toss generated quite a stir. Or, for those who appreciate rugby, scrum.

✧

OUR MOMS CAN'T stop talking to each other. I hope they moved beyond potty training and at least are up to puberty. Especially since they believe Deb and I are about to lose our virginity tonight. Deb because she's a good girl. Me because, well, it's me.

✧

"NO CAKE IN the face." This is Deb's first order as a wife.
Smoosh.
"Through right and wrong," I remind Deb.
In total, Deb and I manage to eat three bites of dinner and one forkful of cake and share three glasses of champagne and six vodka tonics. There was just never time to relax. Except for a brief moment when we sneak out to higher ground to observe the party in action.
"Nice shindig," I commend Deb.
"You could have helped," Deb lovingly states.
"Through better or worse," I remind Deb.

✧

I AM ABLE to sneak out with my buddies during the Macarena (damn, I did forget to veto that one). One thing being married hasn't done is change my gambling luck. I stop after losing fifty dollars.
We do the traditional Jewish chair dance. I pity those lifting me up. Forget the rain insurance, I hope my personal insurance covers friends' hernias. I never saw my parents happier than when they were raised up in the middle of the dance floor.

Married people tend to let loose at weddings. Even more so than single folks. Dancing like they're being judged by Dick Clark. Or Don Cornelius. Is it because they are happy to welcome a new member to the married demographic? Glad to be away from their kids for a few hours? Ecstatic that they aren't paying for this affair?

DEB SURPRISES ME by stepping up to the microphone to say a few words. Besides thanking everyone for coming, she thanks me for what I said to her on our first date.

"And then Craig said that I was so beautiful," she tells the crowd.

Looking back, Deb must have thought how special that was for me to say.

Looking back, I am thinking that I was just telling her the truth.

"But what really did it was when he said that I wasn't just beautiful on the outside, but on the inside as well," Deb adds. "That's how I knew he was the one."

How could my speech top that?

"First of all, I'm not that cool," I open with.

"You got that right!" Drew shouts out.

Again, Drew, the Roast Craig train left the station long ago.

I thank Nick for Deb's number. I thank Deb for calling me back. I thank my parents for supporting me. I thank Deb's mom for supporting Deb. I thank everyone for supporting me on the chair. I thank Deb again. For being so beautiful (I don't mind stealing from her speech). And for marrying me. And for planning the wedding. And for . . .

THE RECEPTION WINDS down. Time to load the guests on the buses. And here's when our picture-perfect wedding comes crashing down. Confusion. Riots. Looting. It's not that bad, but I have to convince everyone that while it's nice to hang around, time's up. Or at least the open bar is now closed. It's nice to know they are all having such a good time that we have to pry them out of here.

"Only two buses and they're pulling out!" I announce.

With no room left on either bus, Deb, Jake, Jon, and I take a cab back to the Strip. We stop in front of the Welcome to Fabulous Las Vegas sign for a few more pictures. And waves to the honking cars passing by. A truly Vegas moment.

✧

THE BEAUTY OF Vegas is that you could be on your last penny or Cloud Nine (or both, like us), and there's always a party going on. We spend the next several hours dancing and having a blast at the casino bar in Mandalay Bay.

Deb jumps on stage with four other brides and shakes it to "We Are Family." All the gamblers, hotel guests, and staff stop to congratulate her. Her wedding dress is a praise magnet. Free drinks. Free hugs. Free kisses. Me? My tux is a magnet, too. Not for praise, but for casino information.

"Where's the bathroom?"
"Is there an ATM here?"
"Aren't you my lousy blackjack dealer?"

We dance until our feet hurt. I don't care if I dance badly now. I'm married. The waistline will go next. We finally call it a night around four in the morning.

"Our first threshold," I whisper as I carry Deb into the elevator.

We kiss all the way up to the thirty-sixth floor. Deb still in my arms as we pass through the doors again. "Our second threshold."

Down the hallway to our suite. My legs start to buckle ever so slightly.

"Guess you should have planned this threshold thing a bit more?" Deb jokes.

"Threshold three," I grunt and toss Deb onto our bed, which has been decorated by our loving bridal party. Half in red and white M&Ms (no doubt the girls) and half in casino chips (no doubt the boys).

"I'm glad we didn't elope," is all I can say in between our kisses. A far cry from just twenty-four hours ago.

SAVING YOURSELF FOR THE WEDDING?
YOU AREN'T ALONE. JUST READY TO EXPLODE.

One in six men are virgins
on their wedding night

Two in six women are virgins
on their wedding night

One in eight men don't have sex
once on their wedding night

Two in eight men have sex
three or more times
on their wedding night

Two in five men
carry their brides
over the threshold

Source: "A Nice Ring to It," *Men's Health,* June 2002

Married Life.

WHAT HAPPENS IN VEGAS IS LEGALLY RECOGNIZED IN EVERY OTHER STATE.

When two people love each other, they don't look at each other,
they look in the same direction.
(Ginger Rogers)

FOUR AM. I'M awake. Not because I can't sleep. We haven't gone to bed yet.

The party's over. Or has it just begun? I'm not sure whether it's the vodka tonics I just drank (I must thank my mother-in-law), the sudden loss of blood to my head (I must remind myself to lift from my knees the next time I carry Deb over anything), or the pure love coursing through my veins (Or is it just the vodka? No, it's love.), but I get it.

I get Deb.
I get me.
I get the wedding.
I get all of the planning fuss.
I even get most of the planning muss.

✧

My advice to any guy getting married who asks and even those who don't is to take a deep breath and dive right in. Seek out the fun in the plans. Don't be scared of the enormity of the tasks that lie ahead. That'll only scare you silent. And silly. Focus on a few things and do them as well as you would do any project. Your fiancée will take care of the rest. I promise. If you don't step up, she will and then you'll be like me. A (loosely defined) man realizing he will be apologizing for quite some time. Especially when the pictures are shown, videos projected, and stories shared.

✧

"I'm sorry Deb," I begin. "I should have helped more. You threw a wonderful party and I was just along for the ride. How can I ever repay you, Mrs. Michaels?"

From the look on Deb's face, I don't think the Mrs. Michaels thing has fully taken root.

"Well, Mr. Michaels, we do have our husband-and-wife brunch tomorrow morning. Nine AM. Think you can plan on being there?"

"Nine? After what I'm about to do to you, I don't think we'll be getting out of this bed until next Tuesday."

We kiss. We feed each other M&M's. We laugh. I eat more M&M's. We undress. I eat more M&M's. We consummate our marriage.

So, I probably took longer consuming than consummating, but what's done is done. And what's done is me.

✧

Our post-wedding brunch is a bit blurry, but Deb and I manage to walk hand in hand around the room to thank everyone, take pictures, and hug some new relatives.

Not that I want to do last night all over again, but it was really a once in a lifetime moment. One that everyone should get to experience. And cherish. It doesn't have to be in Vegas. Or cost more than an Ivy League education. Or have more people than an army battalion. It just has to be special for you and your true love. In fact, the more simple you keep it, the more special it might actually be. Friends, family, and some food.

I GUESS MY guys are too busy gambling to eat, but Deb's crew is right by her side, still supporting their leader. And while maybe we're not the most coherent at this hour, Deb and I are the happiest we've been in a long time. And why shouldn't we be? In a few hours, there's a flight to Hawaii waiting for us, fruity cocktails chilling at a beachfront bar, and a king-size bed waiting for us to give this whole marriage thing a whirl. Our quickie last night notwithstanding.

✧

THIS REALLY HAPPENED. Just like I am glad I had my proposal caught on tape, I want to share with the world how I went from wannabe happy-go-lucky bachelor to definitely-be happier-and-luckier husband. To Deb, getting me excited about our engagement must have felt like pulling teeth, and truth be told (in case you haven't figured this out by now), I wasn't the most supportive or comforting. But, in retrospect, it was a fun adventure. One that's only truly getting started.

"What about our first Thanksgiving? Our first baby? Our first high school graduation? Our first college graduation? Our first child's wedding?" I ask Deb at thirty thousand feet.

"Oy vey!" Deb exhales.

Guess Cousin Isaac got his wish after all.

WISH ME LUCK!
-CRAIG

THE COMPLETE GUIDE TO
THE GROOM'S WEDDING TO-DO'S

Groom To-do's	Details
36+ months before wedding	
Find perfect match	On average, you'll date the girl of your dreams three years before proposing.
	If you are single or just starting to date, you have time. So why are you reading this? If you have been dating for a while, watch the clock. You can bet she is.
Survive third date	If you clear this hurdle, there is generally nothing stopping you. For some reason, she likes you. Don't blow it.
24 months before wedding	
Please girlfriend	By now, she should have had at least a handful of orgasms. If not, maybe you should consider picking up a few power tools at your neighborhood adult store.
	Having a healthy sex life is important, especially at this point in your relationship. It only goes downhill from here. A recent survey found that married couples have sex thirty percent less often than unmarried couples living together.
18 months before wedding	
Please her parents	Sooner or later, you're going to meet her parents.
	Be polite. Be respectful. After all, you can have rude, disrespectful sex with your girl-

GROOM TO-DO'S	DETAILS
	friend once dinner with your future in-laws ends. Just make sure they actually leave the restaurant before you go at it in the restroom.
Start saving pennies	It's coming. You know it. She knows it. And most important, Sal, the discount jeweler who advertises on late-night television, knows it.

16 months before wedding

Please your parents	Don't abandon your folks. Take her home for Thanksgiving. And if you have family issues or cultural differences, make sure to prep her ahead of time. For example, if you're Jewish and she's not, try slipping matzo ball soup into her recipe file, extolling the benefits of eight days of presents in December, and making sure she knows "it's not a beanie."

13 months before wedding

Pick out engagement ring	This is a big step. And, if you're feeling generous, a bigger purchase than your car. Regardless of your means, bump up your budget. She's going to look at the ring every day. Sooner or later, it'll pay off.
Propose	Think you're done now? Think again. Then read on . . .

12 months before wedding

Discuss expenses and budget	The average wedding costs around $26,000. And lasts about four hours. Do the math. Wait. Don't do the math.
Pick out location	Compromise is the cornerstone of any relationship. So don't be too stubborn when she objects to a wedding at a Star Trek convention.
Choose best man and ushers	In ancient times, groomsmen provided the muscle necessary to complete a marriage. In modern times, groomsmen are more likely used to entertain single bridesmaids. Or keep you out of too much trouble.
Endure countless wedding vendor visits	In order to stay in her good graces, be prepared to attend plenty of bridal fairs,

food tastings, music listenings, and wedding planner interviews.

Remember being prepared to go does not imply being prepared to offer an opinion. Speak only when spoken to. And if asked, "I like what you like" is always a safe response.

---

9 months before wedding

Start guest list	The average number of guests invited to a wedding is one hundred and sixty four. So start making new friends or digging up old relatives if necessary.
Help choose bridal registry	Dizzy from china patterns? Don't believe you should use a minimum of two forks per meal? Try adding a few items from Home Depot or the Sony store. Not sure how to ask for cold hard cash? There are many online services to help your guests contribute to a honeymoon, home purchasing account, or mutual fund.
Discuss ceremony and counseling with clergy or officiant	If you plan on a religious ceremony, check for pre-wedding requirements, such as couples counseling. If it's interfaith, clear things with your priest or rabbi first. You don't want "I object" to come from the altar. Other than the promise to marry, the content of the ceremony is yours to make up. Be creative!
Start honeymoon plans	This one is all you! She expects you to plan this. From Airline tickets to Zoo tours. The average honeymoon lasts eight days and costs over $3,700. Remember to confirm your passports are still valid and check for any visa or immunization requirements.
Book talent	Music can make or break a party. Spend time scouting for talent. Hit the clubs. Crash a few weddings. At a minimum, make sure the band can play the songs you most want. A DJ choice is usually less expensive and can offer a wider variety of music, but is generally less formal. An iPod with

speakers can work as well, but designate someone else as tech support.

And make sure you get everything you want in writing. You know how flaky rock stars can be.

Attend engagement party

The first of many parties to come! This is the time to announce your upcoming union to the world. Invite friends and family, but probably not any ex-girlfriends. Or at least not your most recent ex-girlfriend.

Gifts should be appreciated, but not required. Although you might want to note who brings the fifty-dollar bottle of champagne and who brings the six-pack of sparkling grape cider.

---

6 months before wedding

Complete honeymoon plans

Waiting for that amazing last-minute deal? Unless she's both adventuresome and has a good sense of humor, don't. While you might score a cheap trip to Fiji sixteen hours before you say "I do," there's a good chance you'll wind up on a two-week tour of Cleveland.

Pay for bride's bouquet, boutonnieres, and corsages

Technically, you are responsible for paying for all those flowers. Make sure you take your allergy pills that day.

Plan rehearsal dinner

The groom (or his family) picks up the check for the rehearsal dinner. Choose a fun place, such as a restaurant or a large house, to celebrate. But try not to invite the world.

Typically, you should invite the wedding party, both sets of parents, grandparents and godparents, the officiant, and any out-of-town guests.

Arrange wedding party transportation

The last thing you want to do is leave your best man stranded (despite all the times he hooked up at a bar and left you without cabfare).

4 months before wedding

Find new place to live, if necessary

If you aren't living together already, you need to plan for shelter after the wedding. Your choices are simple: your place, her place, or some place else.

Compare cost, square footage, rodent population, and ability to store things (lots of presents are coming). If you're still undecided, think about neutral territory. Just be sure there's room for your La-Z-Boy, neon Bud sign, and high school diploma.

Take bride away for weekend

By now, your blood pressure may be higher than your ATM limit. You need a break. And don't forget the future Mrs. You need a break, too.

Take a wedding-free trip for the weekend. Don't worry about spending a lot. Just taking a time-out from the daily grind may mean more to her than a suite at the Four Seasons. But if you can splurge, by all means order the seaweed wrap for two.

Attend Couple's Shower

Couple's Showers are gaining in popularity, so odds are someone will be hosting this for you. The good news is that the gifts tend to be less about the bride. But don't think they'll be more about you. Think couple.

3 months before wedding

Order wedding rings

While her wedding band should probably complement the engagement ring, you have many more choices. There's gold, titanium, or platinum. Comfort, fancy, or plain bands. Diamonds or two-toned accents. Three, four, five, or six millimeters.

If you want different-style rings, you could at least have matching engravings. Some couples have their initials engraved with their wedding date inside the ring. Avoid suggesting "RIP."

Arrange lodging for out-of-town guests

Unless you want your second cousin twice removed staying in your honeymoon suite,

	reserve a block of rooms at a convenient hotel for any out-of-town guests.
Complete guest list	Time to dust off the guest list and keep folks from wondering if they made the cut. If you are tight for space (or cash), prioritize who can bring a date. At a minimum, require each guest to know the last name and ZIP code of his or her intended date. If there are more than a few singles, feel free to help them meet "the one" by putting them at a table together.
Attend dance lessons	Like it or not, you will be the center of attention throughout the wedding. And especially during your first song. If you've been grooving since the term grooving was popular, you might be in good shape. But odds are you need some practice. Find a local dance studio or ballroom that offers wedding packages. Typically they include both group and private sessions. And if you want to swing, salsa, or tango, make sure the instructor is equipped to handle it. As well as your hips.
Call your mother	There's going to be a new Mrs. Smith (or Jones or Bundy) soon. And that might cause some concern with the original one. Thank your mom. Tell her how much her support means to you. And to your future wife (even if they aren't on speaking terms yet). A simple call to mom will help make your transition from her innocent little boy to her married big man easier. Put those free nighttime minutes to good use.
Shop for honeymoon clothes	It's never too early to shop. Unless you are trying to drop a Speedo size or two. But remember, losing weight gets harder as the wedding approaches. And anxieties soar. Plus after all of your wedding expenses, you might not want to go clothes shopping. But before you dismiss a J. Crew trip, consider how much of a mood-blower your tattered Motley Crue T-shirt will be at your five-star beach bungalow.

Groom to-do's	Details
Order wedding attire for self and groomsmen	Technically, a tuxedo is considered semiformal attire, but it's probably what you and your groomsmen will be wearing on the big day. At many tux rental shops, your outfit is free if the wedding party uses the same shop. If your groomsmen are not in the same city, be sure to provide them with a fitting chart for them to get sized at a local shop and then sent to the one supplying the tuxedos for the wedding.
Check marriage license requirements	You should call or visit the appropriate license bureau (usually the city or county clerk's office) and make sure you understand how to obtain a license. You may have to get a blood test in order to complete the application.

Some states have a mandatory waiting period and/or expiration date for the licenses. It's best not to joke about any of these topics with your mate. |
| Select gifts for bride and groomsmen | A gift is a great way to thank your buddies for putting up with you during your engagement and for helping out during the wedding. You could get the same gift for everyone or try to personalize each one. Plan to give the gifts during the rehearsal dinner.

As for your bride, you don't have to go overboard. A simple (read: less expensive than the engagement ring you are still making payments on) piece of jewelry or keepsake (scrapbook or photo album) should do the trick. |
| Write Couple's Shower thank-you notes | The wedding hasn't happened and already you have to say thanks. For what? Maybe presents from your Couple's Shower. Or from your engagement party. Or early wedding gifts.

Put your gift of gab to good work. Still stuck? Just be sure to personalize each one by referencing their present and telling the giver what you plan to do with it. Besides returning it for cash. |

Groom To-Do's	Details
Have bachelor party	You're probably not dreading this one. Reassure your fiancée that she shouldn't be, either.
Pick up wedding rings	Nothing shows your woman that you care about the wedding than helping out with the little things so she can focus on bigger issues (like how many roses there will be on each centerpiece). While you are at the jewelry store, make note of all the diamond bracelets, earrings, and necklaces. Just because you bought a diamond ring, don't think you're done with that precious gem.
Begin financial consolidation	Time to start saying "what's mine is yours." If you haven't already, be prepared to discuss how to handle finances (savings, bills, credit cards, etc.) in the future. Research how to add your fiancée to your bank accounts (or open a joint account) and stock portfolios as well as making her your primary beneficiary for insurance and retirement accounts.
Check under her hood	By this point, she has been 150 percent focused on making sure the wedding goes smoothly and zero percent on everything else, including her car. Surprise her by getting the oil changed. Odds are she forgot that pesky three-month-or-three-thousand-mile rule long ago. And if you don't complain about the condition of her car, she may let you use your dipstick on her. Vroom vroom.

2 months before wedding

Mail wedding invitations	Start stuffing, licking, and stamping! Any guest over eighteen should receive an invitation, even those very familiar with the details (like your parents). Never type or use labels on the outer envelope. Stuffing the invitations should be easy for those good at jigsaw puzzles or the SAT. If your family is nearby, sign them up for the fun, too.

Besides the invite, expect to neatly place a response card, envelope, directions, maps, and tissue paper inside.

1 month before the wedding

Wine and dine her

Plan a wedding-free moment by going to your favorite restaurant. Relive your first date. Or kiss. Or you-know-what. Ask how she's doing. And really listen. Don't race home to catch the end of the game. Or the latest episode of CSI. That's what TiVo is for. And if you don't have a TiVo, add it to your registry.

3 weeks before the wedding

Pour your heart out

Time to write your vows, speeches, and toasts. Or at least copy and paste some sappy words from the Web. If you are writing your own vows, try to include words like *love*, *cherish*, *sacrifice*, *promise*, *infinite*, and *respect*. Avoid *pain*, *suffering*, *one-way*, and *maybe*. And don't expect to just wing the speeches and toasts, even if you are a funny drunk. You are not a funny drunk.

Verify honeymoon reservations

Now's not the time to assume all is well with the honeymoon. Expect the worst. Call the airlines, hotels, tour companies, bars, and boogie board rental shacks. Make sure they know you are coming.

You might want to order flowers, fresh fruit, and champagne to be in your hotel room before you arrive. Or at least save your bag of airplane peanuts. Okay, just steal hers.

Arrange with best man for ride from reception to airport

No, this isn't about a getaway car. Your best man should help with ride arrangements from the reception to the airport (or hotel if you are leaving the next day).

It's okay to rely on your best man for help with other things as well. That's his job. Along with marrying your fiancée if you fail to show up at the wedding.

2 weeks before the wedding

Pick up license

Time to head to the clerk's office and sign your life away. Go as a couple and bring proper identification (document needs to have both your picture and signature). If this isn't your first marriage, be prepared to say when your last one ended. If it's recent, you may need to show a certified copy of the divorce or death certificate.

It shouldn't take too long to complete this task. Do something fun afterward.

Remind groomsmen of rehearsal and wedding details

Besides telling your friends to take it easy on the still-single-and-desperate women guests, you should take the time to explain any special seating requirements or other wedding details. In addition, give the officiant's fee to best man. Preferably in check form. Especially if you are giving your groomsmen's pep talk at a strip joint.

1 week before the wedding

Pack your bags

It's not what you think. Or if you failed miserably at helping her plan the wedding, it is what you think.

Take a few moments and pack a change of clothes for after the reception and all your new honeymoon attire. Doing this early will ensure you have time for some last-minute purchases. You can't have enough flower-print shirts and boat shoes.

Arrange move to new home and change-of-address form, if necessary

If there's any moving to be done, do it now to make easier when you get back from your honeymoon. Throw out the garbage (translation: anything your fiancée says is the "old you"), box your stuff, and coordinate the movers (or the U-Haul truck, if you are a do-it-yourselfer).

Pick up tuxedo

Try on your tux to make sure all the measurements were correct. Or if your weight swung one way or the other, there's enough time to alter the outfit.

Groom to-do's	Details
	Also, follow up with everyone in your wedding party, including fathers, to make sure they pick up their tuxedos as well. Nothing ruins a wedding faster than a group of guys who look like they picked their formalwear from Goodwill.
Upgrade personal hygiene	Time's running out. While you probably won't drop a few inches around your waist or get those six-pack abs she really wants, there are things you can do to be more presentable during your wedding (and beyond).
	Get a haircut. Floss more often. Sleep a bit longer. And a few last-minute workouts, and stomach crunches wouldn't hurt, either.

3 days before the wedding

Attend rehearsal and dinner	Practice makes perfect. Hence the rehearsal. Make sure your fiancée is happy. Now's the time to make any changes (other than changing fiancées).
	The best man and host (usually your father) should make toasts at the dinner. You and your fiancée should thank the wedding party and your parents as well. Also, now is the time to hand out your groomsmen gifts.

Wedding day

Have a big breakfast	Don't be the malnourished groom that passes out from the stress. Be the well-fed groom who can hold his liquor all night.
Get luggage ready	If you're not packed by now, prepare to increase your credit card limits for all those honeymoon hotel lobby shopping you'll be doing.
Give ring to best man	Check for pocket holes first. Don't dig too deep and give anyone doubts on why you are marrying a woman.
Bring marriage license	Ignorance isn't a valid excuse at this point
Turn off cell phone	If the caller is that important, don't you think you should have invited him or her to the wedding?

Groom To-Do's	Details
Don't be late	Even in movies, this move can be fatal.
Say "I do"	And after you affirm your intentions, take a deep breath and enjoy the moment. The best is about to come.
Socialize at wedding	Your guests traveled far and wide to join you today. And even if they didn't, you should still thank everyone for sharing in your special day. Don't just hang with your bride. You'll have the next four or five decades for that. Mingle. Dance with guests. Smile for pictures. Also, eat some food. Most couples forget to enjoy what they spent all their money on.
Speak up	The first few toasts will be about you (from the best man, maid of honor, and your bride's father). Then it's your turn to speak. This is your chance to toast your new bride, thank your families (especially your in-laws), and thank friends for coming.
Seal the deal	Don't go to sleep without officially sanctioning the wedding. And satisfying your new wife. But, if you only get one out of two done, at least you're married. Where else can she go?

THE COMPLETE GUIDE TO THE GROOM'S PARTY RESPONSIBILITIES

Every day's a party. When you're engaged.

Well, maybe not every day, but there are a few days for you to especially look forward to during the engagement. What about after you're married? I won't ruin the surprise.

Engagement party: Tell the world you're off the market.
Don't feel pressured to invite too many people to your engagement party. Also, try not to invite anyone not being invited to the wedding. Usually, you ask close family and friends. Traditionally, the bride's parents host, but it could be the groom's parents or just friends that throw the shindig. Whoever hosts has the honor of making the first toast to the couple. After that, it's open mic time.

This might be the first time your families are meeting, so make sure everyone's happy and swapping embarrassing stories about you and your fiancée, from toilet training to first kiss and beyond.

Gifts are not required for the engagement party.

If you want to submit an engagement announcement to your local paper, be prepared to pay a fee for this privilege. Go to the paper's Web site or try calling the Lifestyle or Community editors for exact details. Besides your names, you'll probably be asked to include information about your educational background, jobs, your parents' names, and where everyone lives.

You can also request a presidential acknowledgment of your wedding by mailing or faxing to The White House Greetings Office at:

The White House
Attn: Greetings Office
1600 Pennsylvania Avenue NW
Washington DC 20502-0039
Fax number: 202-395-1232

Please include the following in your request:
* Married names and home address of the couple
* Wedding date
* Requestor's name and daytime phone number

Requests should be sent to the White House Greetings Office after the wedding. For more info visit, whitehouse.gov/greeting.

Couple's Shower: Don't get too excited, there's no hot water nor soaping up.

This is not a required event, but is often thrown for you. Lots of wedding talk. Lots of party games. And even some gifts. First and foremost, invite your friends. This is a time to relax and enjoy the moment. Don't feel obligated to invite all of your relatives. Of course, you should expect your immediate family to attend.

Be prepared to play games like:
* **Quiz show.** Prior to the shower, people will ask you and your fiancée questions that the other will be asked during the shower. You'll be judged on how well she knows your answers and you know her answers. So start watching her like a hawk. And take notes.
* **Build an album.** Everyone brings a picture of them with you or your fiancée (or both of you) that they will add to a big album while telling the story behind the picture.
* **Sex Ed 101.** Your fiancée is blindfolded, holding a stick between her legs. You hold a cardboard paper roll in between your legs and help navigate your fiancée toward, and ultimately in, you.

* **Thighs-o-my.** You fiancée is blindfolded and has to feel the legs of the male guests, you included. Then she has to decide which one is yours. You can do the same thing with kisses, but insist on no tongues.
* **This is your life.** Someone writes the story of your married life, but removes the details (think Mad Libs). During the shower, your guests fill in the blanks.
* **Sticky fingers.** Guests are presented with a bowl of candies. After they take one, two or a handful, they are then told that they have to tell as many stories about you and your fiancée as many candies they grabbed.
* **Dress up.** You get blindfolded and are presented with a suitcase full of things your fiancée might wear on your wedding night. Without looking, you dress your fiancée as much as you can in two minutes.

Bachelor Party: Your time to shine. Or lurk in a corner.

City suggestions:

Las Vegas	Reno
Vancouver	Miami
Key West	NYC
Tijuana	L.A.
Atlantic City	Montreal

See "Lost Weekend" for more tips!

Rehearsal dinner: The calm (or not so calm) before the storm. Practice makes perfect. You should expect to run through the entire ceremony with all the usual suspects (you, your fiancée, your parents, the wedding party, and anyone else with a role besides crying in their seats). Make sure everyone (including you) knows the details. After the rehearsal, your parents should host the party. Invite your immediate family, the wedding party and their spouses or significant others, and the officiant. You can invite out-of-towners, but if there are too many for the rehearsal dinner, consider throwing a separate (and more casual) party for everyone the night before the wedding. In these cases, move the rehearsal dinner to two days before the wedding.

The rehearsal party could be informal or fancy, but the point is to gather with your families and get excited for the big day. The host, typically your father, should give the first toast. You should thank everyone as well. The party is also a great time to give your gifts to the bride and groomsmen.

Ceremony and Reception: All eyes are on you.
It's time. You can wait at the altar for your bride or be walked down by parents (before the bride enters).

* In Christian ceremonies, your family sits on the right side and you stand to your bride's right.
* In Jewish ceremonies, your family sits on the left and you stand to your bride's left.
* In mixed marriages, toss a coin. And get used to that coin being your religious decision maker.

Legally, other than the promise to marry, the content of the ceremony is yours to write. Be creative, but remember your guests. And the DVD.

Traditional ceremonies have the following order of events:
* You and your best man will be waiting (or you are escorted by your parents), usher escorts bride's mom, groomsmen and bridesmaids, maid of honor, ring bearer and flower girl, and, last but not least, the father of bride with your bride.
* The officiant welcomes everyone.
* Your parents will be asked who gives you and your bride to be married.
* Readings and/or music.
* You and your bride will exchange vows.
* You and your bride will exchange rings (put hers on first).
* Rings will be blessed.

* The officiant will pronounce you husband and wife.
* You and/or your bride will do something special (break glass, light candle).
* The officiant will offer a final blessing.
* The officiant will present you to the guests as husband and wife.
* Everyone heads out to party (you and bride, flower girl and ring bearer, maid of honor and best man, bride's parents, your parents, and then wedding guests).

And for the reception:

* Pictures.
* Cocktail hour.
* Introduction of your parents, bride's parents, flower girl and ring bearer, bridesmaid and groomsmen, maid of honor and best man, and bride and groom.
* First dance.
* Toasts (best man, maid of honor, fathers, groom, bride, mothers, and then anyone else).
* Food.
* Cut the cake.
* Bridal dances (bride with father, groom with mother, and wedding party).
* Bouquet toss.
* Garter toss.
* You and bride thank everyone.
* You carry bride over threshold.
* You consummate the marriage. Twice if you're a real man.

Day-After Brunch: The first omelet of the rest of your life.
If you're still around, invite family and any guests remaining to a casual brunch either at a fun location or a parent's house (not that a parent's house isn't fun). While it is expected that the bride's parents pay, you might want to step up and take care of the check. After all, you are the man of your family now.

Honeymoon: Finally you two are alone. Now what do you do?
Time to break out the his-and-her thongs and enjoy your time as newlyweds.

Of course, you could cut to the chase and just elope. Make sure your fiancée really wants to do this, your families won't be disappointed, and you can bank some of the wedding fund that won't get used. If not, suck it up and enjoy the parties.